Smart
WORK:
The Syntax Guide for Mutual Understanding in the Workplace

Co-authored by:

Lisa J. Marshall & Lucy D. Freedman

KENDALL/HUNT PUBLISHING COMPANY
4050 Westmark Drive   Dubuque, Iowa 52002

Cover design by David Freedman.

Copyright © 1995 by Syntax Communication Modeling Corporation

Library of Congress Catalog Card Number: 95-78046

ISBN 0-7872-0491-9

Printed in the United States of America
10 9 8 7 6 5 4

Endorsements for
Smart **Work**

"Lisa Marshall's and Lucy Freedman's book addresses a subject that is of vital career importance to technical professionals. They effectively address a developmental void that is unrecognized by most technocrats and unfortunately untaught in most technical degree programs."
> —R.L. Fayfich, Director,
> Internal and External Communications
> Westinghouse Electric Corporation

"An extremely useful guide. The manual is practical and written in the language of technical employees. I plan to distribute it widely in our Information Systems and Engineering Departments. It will definitely help our technical employees in Amtrak's quest to become a team centered, customer focused organization."
> —Neil D. Mann
> Vice President
> Human Resources
> Amtrak

"Thank you, Lisa and Lucy, for your expertise, experience, effort and caring to write this comprehensive handbook. I find it a valuable tool for me to use to accomplish the myriad of details and diversity I find in promoting project management and team excellence."
> —Eloise Glasgall
> Manager, Technical Training
> MCI International

"*Smart Work* contains powerful material to help organizations communicate more effectively—saving time and money! Reviewing communication patterns from the 'observation deck' is invaluable advice."
> —Christine R. Day, Ph.D.
> Training Manager
> Big Three Automaker

"*Smart Work* is a detailed guide to saying what you mean and getting others to do the same. Considering how often a failure to do that creates the difficulties technical people face every day, taking seriously the advice in *Smart Work* will save them a good deal of pain. Further, it approaches communication as a technical person would, so its audience will feel right at home with its approach and its style. And they'll learn a lot from it."

—William Bridges, author
Job*Shift*: How to Prosper in a
Workplace Without Jobs

"If I could give a copy of this book to everyone in the world and know that they would all read it and give it their best attention, I could be sure that the world would thereby become a much better place for us all to live in. Quite simply, it is a marvelously detailed set of instructions for how to communicate effectively with others in order to get things done smoothly, efficiently and effectively.

Extremely reader friendly and sensitive to the different ways in which people read things, it should help anyone to be a better team player and successful member of an organization. Though it's clearly slanted toward the business world, it should be generally useful to anyone who wishes to learn how to get along with anyone else, such as a couple trying to make their marriage work better. If I were the head of any organization I would buy this, read it, and then make sure that everyone in my organization also did the same."

—Peter Kline, author
Ten Steps to a Learning
Organization

CONTENTS

PREFACE

Welcome to Mutual Understanding

Question: can *anything* get done unless people share beliefs about what, why and how it should be done? Without shared understanding of the goal, shared beliefs about its importance, and shared knowledge about the current situation, does useful work happen? In short, can anything get done without mutual understanding? We think not. And while this may seem self-evident, any history book reminds us that mutual understanding really is rare.

Why We Wrote This Book

This book is for technical and other professional people who want to increase the frequency with which they establish mutual understanding in their work lives. Its roots go back to 1980, when the current changes in work and the workforce first appeared. As personal computers were beginning to show up on workers' desks, most organizations were already grappling with the application of computer technology: sky-high expenditures, projects two or three years behind schedule, and severe communication breakdowns between the technical experts and everyone else. All from a lack of mutual understanding

Around this time, Lucy Freedman, a management consultant and trainer, was studying various methods for improving communication at work. She recognized that important advances in developing mutual understanding should be applied to handling the increasing demands facing technical and professional people. She also realized that most of the behavioral skills models available at the time were not appreciated by the audience that needed them; anything "touchy-feely" was instantly dismissed.

Freedman developed a technical approach to communication for technical professionals and established Syntax Communication Modeling Corporation to make her methods more widely available. After several years, she was joined by Lisa Marshall, whose background in film and video had prepared her for the challenges of getting teams to effectively transmit information and work together.

Over the last decade, Freedman and Marshall have refined the model and perfected methods for teaching the Syntax of Effectiveness. While they continue to make it available through seminars and consultation, they decided it was time to offer it in book form.

You hold the result in your hands.

Who Should Read This Book?

You should, if you attended an engineering or other professional school since 1965, thinking you had work for life and would be left alone to do it, and have discovered that there is no longer job security nor the opportunity to focus on your work. In short, if over the past two decades your professional world has been turned upside down, if you have felt as if someone changed all the rules and did not bother to tell you, then read on. The game *has* changed and *Smart Work* tells you how to play the new one.

Why *You* Should Read It

Our invitation to you is this: Would you like to find it easier to persuade others of the soundness of your ideas? Spend less time in unproductive meetings? Be less exhausted and frustrated by your interactions with your co-workers and managers? And, just possibly, have more time to do the work you love?

Without mutual understanding, that won't happen. Yet establishing mutual understanding takes time, effort and considerable attention. While most of us manage to do it once in a while, few do it consistently and fewer still *always* do it. The costs of not bothering to create mutual understanding— wasted effort, wasted time, wasted money, sometimes even bitterness and despair—are almost always pain and frustration.

Like changing a tennis serve or golf swing, changing deeply programmed unconscious behavior requires deliberation, discipline, and a strong sense of how much better life will be once you master the new moves. *Smart Work* is a handbook of awareness, ideas, and behavioral moves that do not just tell you *what* to do, but *how* to do it. It can increase your power to generate the solid understanding that allows professional efforts and careers to move forward productively.

We are assuming, by the way, that you are already doing a lot of what you will read here. You would not be where you are if you were not capable, both technically and interpersonally. You do it unconsciously, however, and therefore do not have a way to notice when it is not working, let alone fine tune or improve it. The good news: By becoming conscious and deliberate about effective behavior you need not be a victim again of breakdowns in mutual understanding.

How to Read *Smart Work*

Some readers want to get the big picture before they settle down to nuts and bolts. Others like to dip in, try something out, and return if they are convinced of its value. Still others want to start systematically at the beginning and work their way through to the end. Others may just want to have this guide around in case they get in trouble.

Smart Work is organized to accommodate all these styles. You choose what works for you. Each chapter contains a short introduction, a purpose statement to help you decide if it is of interest or use, a body consisting of short sections with topic headings, and a conclusion. Here is how the book flows: We start with a quick review of *how* the game has changed, what has happened to technical and professional work in the last decade. We discuss how your belief system affects your experiences at work. We then introduce a model, based on research about what belief systems and behavior make people effective, that you can use to enhance your technical and professional work. Our model addresses skills in **planning, linking, informing, learning,** and **balancing focus and flexibility.**

Then, the nuts and bolts: Chapters Four through Ten describe powerful behaviors for building and supporting mutual understanding, with case studies and examples. This is where you study "the differences that make the difference" in the New Workplace Game and determine what changes would benefit you the most. We describe dozens of specific actions that you can add to your repertoire, each of which builds and reinforces mutual understanding.

Chapters Eleven and Twelve address the fundamentals of learning which can help you take in and use *Smart Work's* tools and techniques. These are important theory chapters, and, if you learn best by having the big picture, you may want to read them *before* the nuts and bolts section. Then we look at requests and agreements, the fulcrums of mutual understanding, in Chapter Thirteen.

Chapter Fourteen explores the wide range of practical applications of this material offered by the current team environment. Then *you* write the conclusion of the book in Chapter Fifteen through a series of worksheets that get you focused on maintaining balance and developing new skills. Throughout the book are exercises, short case studies, opportunities to think and reflect on the patterns of your own behavior, and suggestions about ways to bring the new behaviors into work situations.

Choosing to Learn

It has been our experience that technical and professional experts have excellent learning strategies—*if* and *when* they are convinced something is worth learning. Building a foundation in mutual understanding is often considered "soft" stuff, not worthy of attention. In fact, it may be the hardest and most important work of all. *Smart Work* is based on fundamental principles about human communication and human behavior, principles that will hold up no matter how much the world keeps changing around us.

So, just as you would enthusiastically approach something that kept you abreast of the latest technical developments in your field, consider what *Smart Work* has to offer. If you choose to use it, the information here will enrich your professional (and personal) life, smooth interactions, and ratchet your stress level down several notches. While these skills cannot slow the rate of change or guarantee your job indefinitely, they can provide new personal capability, flexibility, and career satisfaction. The time and energy you invest in learning how to "work smart" won't be wasted on skills that become obsolete in six months. It is your best investment for the turbulent transition to the twenty-first century.

The Authors

ACKNOWLEDGMENTS

"If we'da known how hard this was going to be, we probably never woulda started." No doubt most authors feel the same when the writing process ends. Finishing a book engenders many feelings: relief, pleasure, a slight disorientation, and ultimately, a profound sense of gratitude. Gratitude both for the clarity and focus that the writing process has forced, and for all those who have contributed along the way. In our case, the contributors fall into the categories of sources, clients, helpers, family and friends. And, of course, those who fall into multiple categories.

In the category of **sources**, Chris Argyris, Richard Bandler, Eric Berne, William Bridges, Robert Dilts, Fernando Flores, John Grinder and Meg Wheatley have offered inspiration and insight that has profoundly enriched our understanding of the world and how to move effectively within it.

Our **clients** have been partners in and the source of our greatest learning over the years. Special thanks go to Jim Campbell and George Cavell of the US Postal Service, Paul Hardt of IC System, Roberta Amstadt, Kathy Braglia, Ned Brown, Lynn Potts and Stan Wheeler at EDS, Ron Crough at Hewlett-Packard and Nancy Wong at Pacific Gas & Electric.

Throughout the process, **friends** have encouraged, supported and exhorted us forward. Some have plowed (and we do mean plowed) through early drafts and suggested the kinds of pruning and clearing that only friends can suggest. We're especially grateful to Sue Bethanis, Gene Calvert, Sandy Mobley, Larry Solow and Nancy Wong for both the feedback and the support. Ken Scharf gets special thanks for gently badgering us to communicate clearly about the process of communicating.

Family, of course, bore the brunt of this process. Husbands, children, siblings and parents were all enlisted at various points, both for feedback and support. Our parents gave us the deep and abiding appreciation of and respect for excellence in communication that is the root of all our work. Our husbands and kids gave us day-to-day support, meals alongside the computer and forbearance as we labored on. We thank them, one and all: Larry, Scott, Ginger, Melissa, Stan and Martha, Stan and Alice, Ann, David, Edie, Dianne and Laurie.

Helpers include all those whose professional expertise we enlisted over the course of this process: Rick Crandall and Terry Fischer, whose editing insights were invaluable to the degree of clarity this effort finally achieved;

Linda Kirste, who labored diligently on copy edits and index entries, and Ray Herndon, whose patience through a variety of trials and tribulations was noteworthy indeed. Thanks to all of you.

And then, finally we give thanks to and for each other: for partnership, for patience, for diligence and perseverance, for loving and not letting go. For struggling to be people who do all the things in this book, and for forgiving each other when we don't always make it. We are grateful to have each other as business partners and lifelong friends.

CHAPTER ONE

The New Workplace Game

In the last decade, major corporations have laid off millions of middle managers. "Yes," you may be thinking, "but technical skills are still needed." This may be true, although not as certain as it was a few years ago. What may not be as obvious, however, is that *somebody* needs to do many of the things those millions of middle managers were doing. Since you are the only ones left, guess what? "No fair! That's not what I want to do, and besides, I don't do it all that well. I *chose* the work I'm good at!" It may not be fair. And it may not be what you are good at. It is, however, what is happening. Furthermore, the chances that those managers will be re-hired are nil.

Purpose

The purpose of this chapter is to look at what has brought us to this point, how the nature of your work has changed as a result, and the implications for your career. We will explore the New Workplace and identify the behaviors that will help you succeed there.

The Change

In the preface we described how most of us sense that the game has changed, and no one is telling us the new rules. The world has changed, pretty dramatically. Here are just a few of the changes that have occurred in your lifetime, many since 1980:

- From 1955 to 1980 we saw three generations of computers; from 1980 to 1992, we saw five more; and expect to see seven more by the end of the century.[1] Each generation shrinks in size and increases in power. In 1980, almost no one used a personal computer. In 1995, most educated adults in the U.S. did. We now routinely carry around in our briefcases the computing power of a mainframe computer of twenty-five years ago.

---

[1] *Technical & Skills Training Magazine*, April 1993, 15.

- In the 1950s, the average thirty-year-old in the U.S. spent 14 percent of gross income on the mortgage; in 1973 that was up to 21 percent. In the next decade it climbed to 44 percent. From 1977 to 1989, college tuitions more than doubled for state schools and tripled for private schools in the U.S.[2] The rise continues unabated. The U.S. was ranked second in average per capita income in 1987; by 1990 it was fifth.[3]

- The working half-life of the knowledge of an electronics technician has shrunk from ten years in the 1970s to five today; by the year 2000 it will be halved again.[4]

- Since 1982, four million jobs were cut out of Fortune 500 industrial companies. For the first time in U.S. history, unemployed white collar workers outnumber unemployed blue collar workers.[5] The temporary agency Manpower is the single largest employer in the country, and small businesses generate most of the new jobs.

Scanning the forces at play in the business environment, we see four trends that have changed the nature of work forever:

- **The global economy** is creating an ever-sharpening edge to competition. Success in the '90s and beyond may be defined as survival. The bottom line won't be just quality or service excellence or leanness or technology or time-based competition: It will be a combination of all these factors. And more.

- **The span of effort is rising:** More is being demanded of everyone, not just you. We all have to learn more and then "do more with less." The definition of a "world-class operation" is now one that accomplishes the most in the least amount of time, using the least number of resources while delighting the customer. Competency requirements are also changing, and the emphasis is on effective learning.

- **Organizational restructuring will continue.** As companies rethink and re-engineer the way work gets done, old processes are being drastically simplified or outsourced. Businesses of the future will assemble crackerjack teams for specific purposes and then disband them, as film studios do now. Companies will also engage in fluid strategic partnership arrangements, which will shift as the market changes. As a result, *the meanings of "success"*

---

[2] "Living Standards: Running to Stand Still," *The Economist,* 10 November, 1990, 19–22.

[3] *Pittsburgh Post Gazette,* 31 December 1989.

[4] *Technical & Skills,* op. cit.

[5] Jack Gordon. "Into the Dark: Rough Ride Ahead for American Workers," *Training Magazine,* July 1993, 23.

and "career path" are changing radically. The assumption of regular promotions is going the way of lifetime employment. There is not likely to be much "up" in the survivor organizations—they will be flat, flexible and fast—and people will move around a lot.

- **Workforces are increasingly diverse.** Technical workplaces look like the United Nations these days, with men and women from all over the world working closely to build the next generation of whatever it is they do. That was not true twenty years ago, and adds another layer of troubling complexity to daily work.

Despite these huge changes, one thing remains the same: human nature. Fundamental needs, especially those for identity, security and stimulation, are not changing. And the basic similarities and differences between people are not changing, even though the contexts are. The implications of this will be explored throughout the rest of *Smart Work.*

Change Drivers

What caused all these changes? While there are as many theories as there are economists and consultants, certain forces are clearly key drivers.

One is the development of **global companies,** companies which produce global products for local markets and which locate their headquarters anywhere in the world and equidistant from all markets. Global companies are important not for what they individually produce, but because they have changed the rules of competition. They are, in many cases, the creators of the New Workplace.

Another force is the **shift to knowledge-based work,** due to the speed and ease with which information is now transmitted worldwide. An increasingly tangled web of connections is the result. A hacker in Ithaca, New York, angry at his father, shuts down computers nationwide. Lockerbee, a tiny village in Scotland, receives a hailstorm of burning debris because of a religious war fought thousands of miles away. Small changes in one place are magnified hugely elsewhere. The business press characterizes this turbulent reality as **"permanent whitewater."**

Underlying these changes is one inescapable irony: Technology is the root cause of this upheaval, and many readers of this book helped engineer it. Change does not occur in a vacuum: every time a process gets refined, software coding makes the leap to the next generation, mechanical processes get automated, medical advances occur or science discovers a new, better, stronger, lighter building substance, the game changes for someone, somewhere. Eventually those changes trickle back to the most personal levels of how we live our lives and feel about ourselves and our work. No one can predict the enormous consequences for society, nor what new skills we will have to learn.

What This Means to You: The Changing Nature of Work

Until the Industrial Age, people just worked. They did whatever needed to be done, and took however long was needed to do it. Even within specialized trade guilds, there was a completeness to work—you understood everything, and could do everything, even though you might have a specialty. That did not mean there were no time crunches and crises: Ever been on a farm during haying season? It just meant that the rhythm of the work was dictated by the nature of the work itself, and that everyone understood how his or her piece related to the entire process.

Change expert William Bridges has commented that today "most people think of the organizational world as a pattern of 'jobs' the way that a honeycomb is a pattern of those little hexagonal pockets of honey." Based on the last seventy-five years, that is not an unreasonable understanding of the organizational world. The transition we face in the last years of the twentieth century is away from "jobs" and back to "work."

Bridges proposes a new theory about work: that organizations are "great wide fields of 'work needing to be done.'" If one understands work as a field that incorporates whatever elements of human and technological input are needed to produce new service-based products, then clearly thinking in terms of "jobs" becomes useless. As Bridges points out, "When the 'work that needs doing' changes constantly, we cannot constantly be writing new job descriptions and launching searches for the right person."

The New Guidelines

What, then, does the knowledge-intensive, service-based organization demand from its employees? What are the new rules, or guiding principles, for individuals in the New Workplace?

There are nine key guidelines that anyone who wants to survive in the New Workplace needs to understand and master. (See Figure 1-1). Let's examine each of them:

1. **Develop Self-Knowledge.** Bridges calls it "D.A.T.A."—an understanding of your own Desires, Abilities, Temperament and Assets—that allows you to position yourself for maximum growth

1. Develop Self-Knowledge
2. Take Self-Responsibility
3. Hold Clear Vision and Values
4. Manage Personal Boundaries
5. Manage Your Behavior
6. Build Bridges
7. Manage Conflicts
8. "Unlearn" and Learn
9. Accept Uncertainty and Take Risks

FIGURE 1-1: GUIDELINES FOR THE NEW WORKPLACE

and contribution. Some leading companies offer their employees "360° feedback," detailing how their bosses, peers and subordinates perceive them. Based on this kind of feedback and your own self-assessment, you can systematically develop self-awareness and self-control. You learn not to dump home frustrations on co-workers. There is no room in the New Workplace to play out unfinished emotional business from the past. Instead, you become what we call "congruent," able to "walk the talk," so that what you say and what you do reinforce each other.

2. **Take Self-Responsibility.** Understand that it is your job to take care of yourself, and no one else's. Employers won't take care of you any more. You are in charge of your career development, your professional growth, and making sure the work you do is the work you want to be doing. Even in the organizations that do place a premium on development, your interests and the organization's may occasionally diverge—it is up to you to take care of your best interests.

3. **Hold Clear Vision and Values.** Your sense of purpose holds you together when the world is constantly demanding flexibility. It is, in essence, your self-definition, the boundaries which contain the core of who you are and what you are about. Clear Vision and Values serve as the compass, the point of reference for your next decision.

4. **Manage Personal Boundaries.** Your organization will not climb up on the operating table and undergo open-heart surgery in your place. Likewise, you need not suffer stress or pain in its place. In the long run, a person with a healthy home life and a broad range of interests has far more options and opportunities for service and survival. Learning how to make effective requests and create viable agreements goes a long way towards helping to keep your boundaries both flexible and intact.

5. **Manage Your Behavior.** Beyond self-control, you must be able to respond sensitively to a wide variety of situations with the most appropriate and effective behavior. This means more than just not responding inappropriately. It means having "requisite variety," the ability consistently to come up with creative, situation-specific responses that generate positive results.

6. **Build Bridges.** The New Work is both knowledge-intensive and people-intensive. It needs bridges built across organizational boundaries, between organizational partners, among team members, and with customers. This is no longer someone else's responsibility; we are all in sales and customer service. We all add to the organization's credibility with its partners, its customers, its community—both shareholders and stakeholders—and its other employees.

7. **Manage Conflicts.** Your own, as well as other people's. Managing conflicts does not mean sweeping conflicts under the rug. It means accepting them as critical information that indicates people do not have a shared understanding of the goals or the process or that what is happening is not working. If you recognize this, you have new resources with which to increase the "robustness" of a solution. You understand how to use the conflict as data and not let it derail the process.

8. **Unlearn and Learn.** Let go of old assumptions and knowledge, and look at every new situation with fresh eyes. In other words, develop the ability to hold your beliefs lightly, to shift mindsets with the grace of Baryshnikov moving from ballet to modern dancing or Marsalis shifting from classical music to jazz. Don't let go of *everything*: your knowledge of human nature and ability to work well with others will continue to stand you in good stead. And your Vision and Values will keep critical boundaries in place.

9. **Accept Uncertainty and Take Risks.** Learn to tolerate ambiguity. Recognize that there is no such a thing as avoiding risks. Not to make a decision can be every bit as risky as making one. In a world of time-based competition, failure to be proactive makes

you reactive, and you still have to move quickly. In Jack Welch's GE—an organization that has decided to take risks in order to survive—managers are now expected to:

- Deliver on any commitment;
- Share GE values;
- Make their numbers;
- Inspire, not force, employee performance.

Consider the amount of risk embedded in those criteria: Every commitment becomes a risk; not "walking the talk" becomes a risk; lack of technical and business know-how become risks; and on top of all that you can't even tell people what to do!

Where This Takes Us

One of the anomalies of our time is that traits that get you to the top— single-minded drive, ambition, ability to disregard others and focus on your goal—often no longer serve you once you are there. As Jack Welch, Larry Bossidy of AlliedSignal, and other remarkable business leaders demonstrate, self-knowledge, the ability to keep learning and changing, the ability to manage your behavior "sensitive to context"[6] are far more critical. Most of the economic and social "givens" we grew up with have disintegrated in the last decade. While it is not yet completely clear what will replace them, new realities about both self and work are emerging.

These nine guidelines require more than "new techniques." They demand a new kind of capability, a new kind of intelligence. This new intelligence is more integrative and broader than the scientific, detached, rational model of the past. Like the New Workplace, it is people-intensive. (See Chapter Eleven for a more detailed discussion of this new intelligence.)

Conclusion

The skills that will keep technical and other professionals alive and afloat during these whitewater times have much less than in the past to do with technical knowledge, intellectual brilliance, or cutting-edge thinking. They will, for better or for worse, involve people skills. The changes in the nature

---

[6] David R. Gaster. "A Framework for Visionary Leadership," in *New Traditions in Business*, ed. by John Renesch. (San Francisco: Sterling & Stone, 1991), 170.

of work and the workplace require that we learn to work together so that we can all give our best. This is going to require the development of new skills, new capabilities, and new frames of reference. And make no mistake: We are talking about job survival. If you want to make it as a professional in the twenty-first century, you will have to master these skills. This may seem risky, however, there is even greater risk if you do not: The world will pass you by.

CHAPTER TWO

A Model for the New Work

The workplace is hard these days. Uncertainty abounds. People are asking, "When is the next downsizing or reorganization? Will I be laid off? Who among my co-workers will go? Will this project get accomplished? Will the company be bought out? How can they ask us to do so much with so few resources? How can we get anything done when everyone feels fearful? How do I design a career path in this chaos? Can I get a job anywhere else?"

Help! It sounds awful! And for a lot of technical and professional people, it *is*. What can you do about it for yourself?

Perhaps more than you think. You can build a new kind of technical expertise, one that gives you resilience and increased success in this New Game.

Purpose

This chapter introduces you to the *syntax,* or *underlying behavioral structure,* of people who are effective—people who are resilient, communicate well, create mutual understanding, accomplish goals and have a good time doing so. In grammar or computing, the syntax is the hidden structure that generates outcomes. Here you get a snapshot of the underlying structure, the knowledge, skills, and attitudes of highly effective people's operating systems. If overviews do not appeal to you until you have had some experience, skip to Chapter Four and come back after Chapter Ten.

We developed the Syntax Model of Effectiveness described in this chapter by studying what effective people had in common, even when they did very different kinds of work. When you understand the underlying structure of effective behavior, you have much more room to maneuver to get the results you want. And, as with any syntax, once you know the rules, you can discover when and how it can be useful to bend or break them. Without that understanding, you may bend or break them inadvertently, and the results can range from unpleasant to catastrophic.

Each part of the model represents a set of distinctions and behaviors. The explanations, examples, and practices in each chapter guide you toward incorporating the skills and distinctions into your behavior. By the end of this book, your "communication operating system" will have received a complete tune-up!

Communication *Is* the New Work

Have you ever changed planes in a large airport? Dozens of passengers rush to nearby phones, grab the receivers, and start punching in numbers. "Oh look, they're all trying to squeeze some work in," you may have thought. Wait a minute! Since when does being on the phone constitute work? Those phone calls actually epitomize the underlying nature of most work today: communicating, building relationships, and sharing information so that agreements can be made and new steps taken. That's what we do when we work. We set shared goals and build agreements, develop relationships, collect and share information, take action, and then start all over again, presumably having learned something in the process.

You are already very successful as a communicator; you wouldn't be where you are now if you were not. You have a high level of effectiveness and a range of techniques and strategies for reaching mutual understanding in different communication situations. Sometimes, however, when things are not working out as you planned, you may need to remind yourself that you *are* highly skilled and effective, and that the results you get are feedback about refinements you still need to make. You are already doing the best you can, given the choices you perceive. *Effectiveness comes from expanding the range of perceived choices.*

Communication Effectiveness: What Is It?

We define communication as *an exchange of information that creates understanding and generates action.* Communication, under this definition, does not occur unless there is a response. Effectiveness means *producing a desired effect or result.* Effective communication means the response achieved was the response desired. It is a rigorous standard: Intention does not matter. Results do.

Consider professionals whose technical skills and competencies are undermined by their communication skills. They confuse or garble what should be straightforward and simple. Or fail to recognize the impact of their behavior and thus fail to notice that their actions contradict their messages.

Then consider those who are most effective, as team members or leaders, project heads, or managers. While some of their excellence stems from their technical skills and experience, much of their effectiveness comes from their wide range of choices about *how to communicate what they know and how to learn* from others.

The implications of the New Game discussed in Chapter One are profound in this regard. People skills are no longer just for those who get into management. The New Workplace demands dual attention foci; attention to technical knowledge and to the relationships that apply and utilize that knowledge. It demands a quantum leap in interpersonal awareness.

Studies of people who are effective (achieve results, have an impact, make a difference in the world) show that even though their fields of endeavor may be wildly different, they have remarkably similar "operating systems." Of course, those people are usually unaware of how their operating systems work, because operating systems function primarily at an unconscious level. When you ask how they achieved those remarkable results, they usually give you their "application software" answer, the part of their programming they have consciously installed.

For example, one first-rate salesperson describes three questions she always asks because she believes that's what makes the sale happen. Another equally effective salesperson tells about the five ways he asks for the sale, believing that is what makes him so effective. In fact, they both unconsciously establish very strong rapport with their customers, and their specific sales tools have far less impact than that rapport. The Syntax Model of Effectiveness illuminates the "operating system" of effective people and helps *you* learn how to make the distinctions that make *them* so effective.

The Syntax Model of Effectiveness

Our model reflects the patterns of people who get things done with others. Think of it as a mobile hanging so delicately balanced that every passing breeze sets it moving in another direction. This illustrates the important concept that effectiveness is a finely tuned response to the current situation. Effectiveness here is presented from the standpoint of the individual communicator, what *you* need to do to communicate effectively with others. The model includes all the elements necessary and sufficient for effective interpersonal interactions. It does not specifically coincide with classical models of communication, e.g. that there is a sender, a receiver, and a message. We avoid extra theories, rules, or constructs that may be interesting but do not lead directly toward *effectiveness*.

LINK

PLAN   BALANCE   LEARN

INFORM

DYNAMICS OF SYNTAX

FLEXIBILITY
FOCUS

FIGURE 2-1: SYNTAX: STRUCTURE OF EFFECTIVE COMMUNICATION

The model's basic assumptions are that when you communicate with somebody else:

- You have a reason for doing so, whether you are aware of it or not (**PLAN**);
- You need open lines of communication for exchanging information (**LINK**);
- To bridge communication gaps, you need to ask questions and make statements (**INFORM**);
- In every type of communication, feedback is the key to learning (**LEARN**);
- You always face the dilemma of balancing focus on goals with flexibility for meeting the needs of others and the situation (**FOCUS, FLEXIBILITY**); and
- You engage in a give-and-take, based on your requests and agreements (**BALANCE**).

The model is explored in detail in subsequent chapters; here we will offer a brief overview. While we must discuss the model in a linear fashion, we do not imply that there is a predictable step-by-step progression to effectiveness. Instead, the message of the model is that all key elements must be in place before an interaction can be effective. The sequence is not as important as the fact that, *if* any *element is missing, the interaction will be flawed and its impact diluted.*

The **PLAN** aspect of the model addresses the critical issue underlying the detailed planning processes commonly used in engineering and other professional environments: *having a clear goal and knowing why you have it.* We know of instance after instance where huge efforts and detailed plans failed due to lack of this clarity. Establishing mutual understanding about goals is one thing people who are effective *always* do!

The **LINK** aspect includes *establishing rapport with people and handling resistance* in positive and productive ways. When we think of someone as having good people skills, these are the skills we mean.

The **INFORM** aspect concerns the skills of *getting and giving good information*—information unclouded by personal bias, filters, or limiting beliefs. The skills of INFORM are critical for people working in information-saturated contexts where they need to make sense of huge amounts of data.

The **LEARN** aspect is arguably the most important of all. Learning how to learn is *the* core competency in the New Workplace. We define learning as *taking action, noticing the results you're getting, and doing something dif-*

ferent if you are not getting what you want. People who keep doing the same things and expect different results are not learners. The more you increase your ability to learn, the more you can utilize other skills productively and consistently.

The axes of the model illustrate ongoing dynamics. The vertical axis is the **FOCUS** axis. Think of it as a cybernetic loop: Set goal, take action, notice results, adjust. If you have had quality training, the "Plan, Do, Check, Act" process parallels this. The horizontal axis is the **FLEXIBILITY** axis on which data from the environment is acquired and put to use. It contains the skills and tools you use to notice and respond to your current situation.

Most people have stronger skills along one or the other axis. Those in **FOCUS** are very clear about where they are going and how to get there. They often fail to notice whether anyone else willingly comes with them. Those with **FLEXIBILITY** are sensitive to whether people are "with them," but they may lack clear purpose or direction. The first group gets things done, but few want to work with them and they often generate ill will. The second group is well-liked but often weak on performance.

Balance Is What's Important

Each axis is equally important: The critical issue is finding the **BALANCE** point between them. People who are effective know how to find that balance point. They also know how to reestablish balance when they lose it. They unconsciously scan the model, recognize which elements are weakest, and take the steps necessary to strengthen them.

One tool for establishing and maintaining balance is the ability to make clear and concise requests and to respond to requests in ways that minimize confusion and communication breakdowns. Learning, for example, how to create clear "conditions of satisfaction" serves as a kind of internal gyro, maintaining your balance in the constant tug-of-war between **FOCUS** and **FLEXIBILITY**.

Using the Model—A Case Study

Joanne was the manager of Information Services (IS) for a medium-sized branch of an insurance company. While corporate IS handled the systems for personnel and administration, Joanne's operation took care of processing policies and claims for her branch. Joanne had worked for years to get her part of the system functioning smoothly, working within the branch to get users to enter data correctly, rapidly accommodating individual requests from policyholders, and keeping her management involved in decisions about technical matters.

Then the company decided to integrate the two systems.

Responsiveness was the key to Joanne's style. Normally, she would have accepted the directive and begun to plan the conversion, informing and involving people in her branch from the outset. This time, because of the abrupt way the change had been announced, she found herself feeling quite resistant. Having just been exposed to the Syntax Model, however, she took a step back before calling her branch managers to announce the change.

She mentally moved into the top box of the Model, realizing that so far she had been thinking mostly about what she *didn't* want: conflict with corporate as well as with her own management. She decided to stop paying attention to why the decision was made, the limitations of being subject to corporate control, or corporate's failure to appreciate what she had created. Instead, she asked herself "What do *I* want?" She quickly envisioned having it both ways, a combined system that standardized procedures at the corporate level and still allowed her room to be responsive to the people whose productivity she existed to support.

Asking herself, "What would that get us?," Joanne realized that implementing the new system had potential advantages to both her and her branch management, and cost savings for corporate. There could be even more benefits if they incorporated some of her system's features. "Wow," she thought. "All I did was stop thinking about what I *don't* want and reviewed my goals, and already my perspective is much clearer. Now what?"

Two important issues, she realized: "With whom do I need to link in approaching this situation?" Then: "Who needs to know what? And in what form?"

Many people certainly needed information she now possessed. She recognized that she, in turn, needed some information from both the branch managers and from corporate IS. For example, which of the branch's needs are in flux right now? Can we leverage this opportunity to reduce response time or increase flexibility? From corporate IS: Had they tried to solve similar problems in other places? What were the ultimate goals of combining the systems?

In combining the focus on the goal, the awareness of creating a linkage with other people, and the definition of information needs, Joanne consciously thought through her situation more quickly, clearly and thoroughly than ever before. Especially satisfying was that she had avoided those days of discomfort she usually experienced when confronting a problem.

After her short communication audit, Joanne's work was laid out for her. Following the same sequence in discussions with her manager and corporate IS, she found that each person had different specific interests. She was fascinated by the variations in what people found important.

By the end of her first round of conversations, she had most of the elements she needed to write a short proposal that would include her offer—what she felt her department could do—phrased in a way that satisfied everyone. The writing came easily because she knew what she needed to say to each person, and she didn't hesitate to repeat their own words. She painted detailed pictures of what a successful integration would look, sound, and feel like. Her stress was reduced; she knew this was presold because she had listened so carefully and linked to everyone's needs.

Reflecting on it later, Joanne believed she had saved herself two weeks of misery and probably twice that in implementation time downstream. Making requests of people to get the process up and running was simple and straightforward compared with the normal politics of getting things done. Life sure seemed a lot easier than when she had first heard about the impending systems integration!

Conclusion

As professionals, we all have work—tasks and goals that we organize ourselves to perform—and we all have people with, for, and through whom we do these things. We all have conscious and unconscious tools that enable us to accomplish that work with other people. It is less important to know the details of how others process information than to remember that their ways are different from ours.

What generates accomplishment in the workplace are systematic, conscious techniques that bridge differences and focus combined energy on mutual goals. The Syntax Model encapsulates what is needed to maintain resilience and develop professional skills in the kind of work we do now; the work of communicating for mutual understanding.

CHAPTER THREE

Changing Our Minds

To learn is to change perceptions. In the last chapter, Joanne successfully used the Syntax Model because she had shifted her thinking and was willing to try something new. Before we examine each facet of the Syntax Model in upcoming chapters, here are some aspects of Joanne's shift that can open *your* doorways to learning.

Purpose

Specific ways of thinking and approaching interactions have been identified as characteristic of effective people. This chapter introduces some of those attitudes and approaches. It is "high theory": If abstractions bore you, move on to Chapter Four. If you need to hear the big picture and grasp its implications, however, you will find useful material here.

Mental Models, the Patterns of Our Minds

Present-day business thinkers are much concerned with the concept of *mental models,* the assumptions underlying our thinking. They recognize that the way we perceive and sort things determines how we will experience them. Our mental models control our ability to generate possibilities and our ability to understand one another. Writer after writer acknowledges that learning, change, growth, and survival are all linked to awareness of and changes in mental models. Recognition of mental models—your own and others—is central to success in today's team environment and interconnected global economy.

One reason mental models are so important is that today's technical work is head work. Much has already been written about the New Worker— you—as the "knowledge worker." But what exactly does a knowledge worker *do?* Simply having specialized expertise doesn't constitute work. As Walter Kiechel pointed out in *Fortune,* "Truly understanding the emerging economy takes a change of mind set, or inevitably, of paradigm: from thinking of business as making things, or churning out product, to realizing that it consists instead of furnishing services, even within what has traditionally been thought of as manufacturing."[1] What, then, is the "work" of furnishing services?

Applying Mental Models

As you go on sales calls or check on the status of ongoing work or finish a project, or start a new one, ask these questions:

- Do I have a clear idea of my goal? Do I and the other people involved in this work have mutual understanding about our shared goals and plan?

- Do I pay enough attention to the people with whom I work? Do I take the time to build the relationships and trust needed to move this work forward?

- Have I gathered the information I need to make decisions and get this work done? Have I accounted for my own and others' natural tendencies to delete, distort, or generalize information? Have I conveyed information so it is understood by people with diverse thinking styles?

- Am I consciously learning as I go along, noticing the responses to what I do and adjusting my behavior if they are not the ones I want?

This is the work of "furnishing service," the work of the knowledge worker. It is also an example of applying a mental model, deliberately choosing to operate from a clear mental framework about what is important and what needs to be done. You are already operating from some mental model: Do you know what it is? Most of us do not. Our beliefs about the world tend to be invisible, unless they are contradicted by some experience which forces us to step back and examine our assumptions. People who are effective often have more consciousness about their mental models, and, as a result, are better able to adjust them as needed. They continuously build, develop and fine tune their mental models.

The Mental Model for Effectiveness

Think how much more effective you could be if you regularly did a short audit or analysis (like the one we just described) before assuming any job was completed. Indeed, if you kept checking as you went along, you would save hundreds of hours and thousands of dollars in wasted time and effort on nearly every project. Notice also that if you neglect any one of these

---

[1] Walter Kiechel III, "How We Will Work in the Year 2000." *Fortune*, 17 May, 1993, 48.

elements the job does not get done right: You must do all of them to effectively complete a unit of work.

Our Model of Effectiveness (Figure 2-1) describes a unit of work in the New Workplace, the same way "attach bolt A to point B" describes a unit of work on the assembly line. You can use the model to check that a job has been done correctly and completely, or, like Joanne, to diagnose what needs to be done. It provides you with a mental model of the syntax of good work in the New Workplace.

Personal Syntax: The Pattern of Your Behavior

Mental models generate behavior from a complex set of variables. Since humans are self-maintaining organisms, each move we make reflects what we consciously and unconsciously believe will enhance our well-being. Since we usually are not aware of mental models or the assumptions and beliefs they contain, other people's behavioral choices may not make sense to us. Just the same, they are also finely crafted choices.

Those mental models are activated by our perceptions, the information gathered by our senses. Within the bandwidth of our perceptions, we make many distinctions and recognize a vast array of minute differences. We detect many shades of green in the leaves of a tree. A slight, unusual sound at night captures our attention despite all the other sounds going on. We sense relatively tiny changes in the way someone carries himself or herself and in our own physical and emotional states. Our perceptions reflect the way these distinctions register on us.

Each of us is quite selective about the distinctions we make. We care about making some of them, and not about others. Our abilities have developed accordingly. Our experience results from the way we shift attention among different perceptions. We each have a unique perceptual structure, or syntax, within which we operate. Within that structure, we have different strategies for processes such as accessing memories, convincing ourselves, motivating ourselves, making decisions, being creative, and learning.

Playing with Perception

The way you perceive some things and overlook others is the part of your personal syntax that determines what information is available to you. The beauty of individual perceptions is that they create such rich potential. Whenever you vary your behavior, your perceptions change and other possibilities emerge.

For example, try slowing way down. When you slow down, you can pay in-depth attention to what is around you. You have a heightened awareness of—and more information about—feelings and textures and colors and movement and sounds. The details become richer and more powerful. Now speed up. Step out of yourself and observe yourself from outside. Move quickly through the same amounts of information without that detailed awareness and with less sense of feelings or colors, not noticing the sounds at all. You can scan more broadly and quickly, and the finer grain disappears.

These shifts in attention control the scope and detail of the information that is consciously available to us. All of us habitually notice some forms of data more than others, therefore we always have different perceptions to exchange. Some of us always pay attention to the same things, while others are more flexible and can contextualize their perception level for the situation at hand.

Thinking about Thinking

The architecture, or main structure, of a computer operating system is comparable to the role played by an individual's perceptual pattern, or syntax. Our syntax is the way we operate in the world. When closely examined, it illustrates the root of our behavioral patterns, our assumptions about how the world works, what is important, how people do (and should and will) behave. Syntax generates automatic responses to situations.

When you interact with a computer, the primary things that you see, hear, and feel are specific features of the application software, not the operating system in which it is embedded. People experience each other in much the same way. They see the behaviors and hear the words, not the syntax. Unless, of course, intuitively or through training, they know how to access the operating system. Then they can make informed and precise choices about managing the interaction of their syntax with that of others. This is the primary skill of the effective communicator.

Your Learning Syntax

Your learning strategy is the underlying structure of your learning process. It forms your learning syntax—the structure an experience must have for you to learn from it. Just as knowing the rules of baseball or football or chess makes playing the game more satisfying, knowing your own learning strategy can make work life more satisfying. It tells you how to position yourself in any given situation in order to learn the most from it.

Adult learning theory presupposes that grown-ups learn best by doing (as do most children). This has proven especially true for learning behavioral skills: They must be practiced in order to be acquired. However, the stage at which the "doing" occurs can vary considerably. Some people need to comprehend theory before they try something; some need to "do" first and then get theory. Some need to watch, some need to listen, some need to walk through it and have the experience first. Some can anticipate, and some people need a "whack on the side of the head" to notice what they should be learning.

A quick review of a recent learning experience will tell you a lot about *your* learning strategies. What did you do first? Then what happened? What next? What helped your learning? What hindered it? Keep these supports and constraints in mind as you read and experiment with the material in *Smart Work*. Then you can design your own learning experiences. You can also learn to observe your own mental models at work.

The Map Is *Not* the Territory

We have found four concepts especially useful for building a mental model that supports effective communication. As you read them, notice to what extent they may already be part of your personal syntax.

1. *Perceptions and their representations (our thoughts and how we symbolize them) are not the same as reality.* Reading the menu is not eating the meal. The map is *not* the territory. This was a revolutionary idea in recent intellectual history. Now we may take it for granted and not realize how often we still act as if what we perceive is the whole truth and nothing but the truth. As Will Rogers remarked, "It's not what we don't know that hurts us, it's what we know for certain that isn't so."

2. *My self is not the same as your self.* This is more complex than it at first seems. Obviously, there are differences between you and others. However, much of the time we act not only as if our perceptions are the truth, we act as if others perceive things exactly as we do. Being aware of this concept cleans up many of life's daily misunderstandings. It allows us to own the piece of the perception that is ours and not confuse it with the piece that belongs to someone else. For example, *my* feeling about *your* behavior is my responsibility, not yours.

3. *Attention is best directed toward what we do want, not what we don't want.* Since it's pointless to put energy into what we don't want, a mental model, or syntax, that continually focuses on what is wrong is not very useful. When we work to improve commu-

nication and overall effectiveness, the whole thrust must be to direct attention toward what we *do* want, as individuals, teams, and organizations. By recognizing the choice point, and shifting attention toward shared goals, we save countless hours of communicating about the wrong thing.

4. *We represent our knowledge base to ourselves via the information we take in through our senses.* Understanding how we code the data our senses compile allows us to cultivate the ability to perceive subtle and significant differences in each other's experiences. We examine this powerful ability in Chapter Ten.

Conclusion

For many of us, discovering that we have choices about our mental models can be startling. We may have believed things had a fixed quality, a "way it's s'posed to be" that was permanent and unyielding. While this discovery can be frightening, it also creates a new freedom to more fully realize the potential in every situation. Adopting the mental models—the personal syntax—of people with high levels of effectiveness can make a profound difference in your experiences at work and at home.

The best way to approach this is to field test these ideas for a while. What happens when you do not assume everyone's experiences are the same? Or shift your focus from what you *don't* want to what you *do* what? Notice what happens when you take the time to check your interpretations of reality before acting on them. You will find you are already beginning to reduce stress and increase life satisfaction!

CHAPTER FOUR

It Depends on How You Look at Things: The Power of Frames

One of the most powerful functions of our mental models is to determine what we see, hear, and experience in any given situation. Thus, goal-setting should be preceded by making sure we are paying attention to what we *do* want, not what we *don't* want. Most technological development has come about because someone saw possibilities where others did not. We have to be aware of new possibilities before there is a chance for them to come to fruition.

Purpose

A systematic shift from thinking about what went wrong in the past to what could go right in the future is a powerful tool for resolving issues, effecting change, and raising morale. This chapter begins the PLAN section of the Model. It presents practical, hands-on advice on how to make the shift in attitude, or "frame," from reactive to proactive.

Starting to Work

First, an exercise.

Think of an interpersonal situation which you would like to change. It can be anything, work-related or personal, as long as it contains some element you would definitely like to change.

Answer the following questions about that situation. Answer exactly what the question asks—no more, no less.

First Frame:

1. What is the problem?
2. Why do you have it?

3. Who or what is limiting you or preventing you from getting what you want?
4. Whose fault is it?

What kind of internal response did you have? Make notes about the following, to compare with responses later on.

1. What is your energy level?
2. How do you feel about yourself in this situation?
3. How do you feel about the person or persons involved?
4. What is your level of
   —Motivation?
   —Clarity about the situation?
   —Optimism?

Second Frame:
Examine the same situation through a different frame. Again, answer the questions as written, without changing the language in any way.

1. What is your desired outcome?
2. How will you know when you attain it?
3. What possibilities could assist you?
4. What have you learned from the situation?

After answering these questions,

1. Do you notice any differences in energy level?
2. Do you notice any differences in how you feel about yourself?
3. Do you notice any differences in how you feel about others in the situation?
4. Do you notice any differences in your levels of
   —Motivation?
   —Clarity about the situation?
   —Optimism?

Shifting the Frame

What happened when you shifted the frame? For many, the results are dramatic, even profound. Instead of feeling trapped, depressed, or angry, they feel hopeful, encouraged, or excited about new possibilities. They shift to an empowered state. For a few, the results are mild to non-existent. This is especially likely for those who experience the world in a somewhat detached way.

Some actually find their energy is higher in the first frame because unhappiness and anger generate more steam. They may feel more positive about the resolution of the situation after the second frame because they have refocused away from what is wrong and toward what could be right.

If these frame shifts did not elicit a strong response, please check: Did you answer the questions *exactly* as they were asked? Often people don't experience a shift because they have unconsciously altered the language to fit *their* frames. They may have answered the first frame question already looking at their desired outcome or they may have stayed focused on the problem rather than possible solutions while they answered the second frame questions. And there are others whose internal language so dominates their thinking that external wording has little impact. In any case, it is equally important to start noticing how *your* word choices affect *others*. Then you have the flexibility to change when they are getting stuck in the negative.

There is no correct response here, just one important point: *Language affects our bodies and our responses.* How we think about a given situation largely determines how we feel and, thus, how we act. To become more resilient and proactive, observe how differently you feel and respond when you explore what you *want* rather than dwelling on what you *don't want.*

The first frame has been called the Problem Frame or Blame Frame. While these nicknames for a past-oriented approach sound negative, the method is a useful way to experience how people have been unhappy in the past. When an individual, group, or organization is stuck in the first frame:

- There is a whiny quality to explanations of current reality;
- Conversations are repetitive, with the refrain of "Ain't it awful?"
- Every statement includes a lengthy rationale, the gist of which is that "It isn't *my* fault";
- It's usually pretty clear whose fault it *really* is;
- Any collusion with covering up the truth about how bad things are and/or how little the speaker has done to change them is also covered up;
- Many exchanges may begin with some variation of "Well, if you hadn't . . ." or "The problem is . . ."
- There is a lot of CYA (cover your ass) behavior memos written, E-mail messages sent—to assign responsibility for the mess anywhere but here.

In general, the Blame Frame is characterized by a victim mentality, and a refusal to take responsibility for *anything*.

Once you've recognized that you—or someone else—are in the Blame Frame, what do you do? Sometimes, nothing. If feelings are running high, people need to vent "ain't-it-awful" feelings or "visit Pity City." The trick to managing those negative feelings is to not stay there too long and risk getting stuck in a cycle of blaming and victimhood. We have seen entire organizational cultures built around the Blame Frame dynamic. Needless to say, those organizations have encountered serious trouble in the turbulent environment of the '90s. Time is eaten up by defensiveness, responsibility is denied, precious resources are squandered, and productivity nosedives.

It is important not to blame yourself while getting out of the Blame Frame. Remember that once it has served its purpose, staying there wastes time and, more importantly, preserves a less-than-resourceful state of mind. Even those caught in Blame Frame patterns rarely intend to be negative. It is just the way things seem to be.

Moving into the Aim Frame

Before we get out of the Blame Frame and into the Outcome Frame or Aim Frame, an important distinction needs to be made. The Aim Frame is not simply about being positive and upbeat. It is about shifting the locus of control away from paralyzing external forces and back to those you *can* control—the ones within your own "response-ability." Moving into the Aim Frame means taking responsibility for what will happen and empowering yourself and others to act, not waiting for others to act for you. The Aim Frame is not about getting your CEO to do something—that is still external to your control. It is about *you* doing what needs to be done, by yourself or with the help of others.

The difficulty for most people is the fear of being threatened or embarrassed when they begin this shift. Chris Argyris, professor of organizational development at Harvard Business School, has observed that *all* human beings behave similarly when threatened or embarrassed. We instinctively hide our sense of threat or embarrassment, we cover up the fact that we are hiding, and then we cover up the covering up. A self-sealing loop is created. In the name of allowing others to preserve their dignity or save face, everyone colludes in the cover-up. Argyris calls these cycles "defensive routines"; and breaking them is learning to "discuss the undiscussable."[1]

---

[1] Chris Argyris, *Knowledge for Action, A Guide to Overcoming Barriers to Organizational Change* (San Francisco: Jossey-Bass, 1993) 134–49.

Argyris uses another set of concepts to describe how learning processes are affected by such dynamics. He discusses two forms of learning: single-loop and double-loop. Single-loop learning occurs when organizations or individuals design actions and get the results they intended, or can correct initial actions and get the intended results. Double-loop learning occurs "when a mismatch between intentions and outcomes is identified and corrected by first examining and altering the governing variables [theory-in-use] and then the actions."[2] Double-loop learning takes place when people explore the root causes of their actions in their beliefs and values. This requires analyzing our own behavior to identify those beliefs and values since, due to "undiscussability," most of us *do not* "walk our own talk."

In the *Harvard Business Review*, Argyris observed that managers often limit what they and others say, in the name of being considerate or keeping morale up. He notes that this deprives everyone of the opportunity to understand and own their behavior and learn from it. He continues:

> *Admittedly, being considerate and positive can contribute to the solution of single-loop problems like cutting costs. But it will never help people figure out why they lived with problems for years on end, why they covered up those problems, why they covered up the cover-up, why they were so good at pointing to the responsibility of others and so slow to focus on their own.[3]*

The New Workplace Game described in Chapter One makes it clear that if organizations are to survive—and we are to survive inside them—more and more of those hard questions have to be asked. What moves can you make to get out of Blame and into Aim once you've recognized what is going on? Several language patterns can be very helpful.

The first is to **state requests in the positive**. Talk about what you *do* want, not what you don't want. As a corollary, get people to focus on the desired outcome, not all the things that are currently wrong. At one large corporation they teach people to say "I wish" and "H2," meaning "how to," rather than negatives such as "I can't."

Another language pattern is to **ask questions that seek detailed, factual answers**. These questions start with "What," "How," or "When." "What has already been tried?" "How have we communicated these results to others?" "What has been the response?" "What else could be done to address the root causes?" "What fears have these efforts evoked?"

---

[2] Ibid.

[3] Chris Argyris, "Good Communication that Blocks Learning," *Harvard Business Review*, July–August 1994, 79.

These questions avoid collusion with the Blame Frame and defensive routines. They shun rationalizations and blaming explanations. Conversely, questions that begin with "Why" invite the sort of defensive behavior we're trying to avoid. "Why" is a good word to avoid if you want to move a situation from Blame to Aim. The negative power of "Why" is explored in Chapter Eight.

"But" is another word to avoid. "But" has the effect of deleting everything that has gone before it. No matter how sincere the praise or support, "but" makes the brain retreat to primal mode: fight or flight. Either way, the chances that the rest of the message will be remembered are slim. A simple substitution of the word "and" makes tremendous difference in how well you're understood.

Once others perceive from your language patterns and non-verbal behavior that you are really listening, you can begin to move towards solutions. "Well, I'm pretty clear about what you *don't* want—now, what *do* you want?" is one way to invite the shift to the Aim Frame. Other sample phrasings appear in Figure 4-1.

These phrases make it clear that you are aware of others' experience and acknowledge its validity. You are not saying that they are wrong, merely that it is important to move into a goal-oriented mode. You can also say, "How can we work it out so that . . . [both needs get met]?" This acknowledges the reality of the problems and the need to resolve them. It also implies that things *can* be worked out.

All these verbal moves are probably already in your repertoire of behavior. However, if you are not aware that you have them, it is hard to invoke them when you need help. As you get better at recognizing the symptoms of the Blame Frame, you will be better able to make a conscious choice to move into the Aim Frame—where effective communicators get positive results.

	understand		point of view		[state
I	appreciate	*your*	situation	*and*	desired
	sympathize with		concerns		outcome]

FIGURE 4-1: AIM FRAME PHRASES

Case History

A steel stamping plant rolled its own sheet steel. Preventive maintenance on the induction heating machines was supposed to be performed once a month and take about eight hours, but the production people were usually too busy to shut down and give maintenance the time it needed. Of course, when the machines broke down there was almost always a red-hot ingot inside, which meant it had to cool off for sixteen hours before maintenance could begin. Traditionally, Production blamed Maintenance, and Maintenance blamed Production.

Finally, the plant introduced a TQM (Total Quality Management) process. One young manager asked, "How is it that we can't afford eight hours for maintenance, but we can afford twenty-four hours for repairs?" After listening to a furious round of blaming, the on-site TQM facilitator asked very specific questions. "Who here has known about this?" "How long has it been going on?" "How did this situation develop?" "What prevented you from doing something about it?"

Answering questions, the group began to see the situation in an entirely new light. Assumptions about other people's motives or needs had been made but never tested, because to do so might have caused someone to lose face or suffer embarrassment. The first time Production had refused to stop for maintenance was because of a scheduling misunderstanding. Rather than admit that he had misunderstood, a supervisor had requested that the run not be interrupted, claiming it was for a priority customer. The next time that customer had a run, Maintenance assumed it could not be interrupted.

From there, things had quickly deteriorated. It soon became "common knowledge" on the plant floor that one did not interrupt runs for maintenance. Economic pressures were forcing continuous runs, so time for maintenance became scarcer and scarcer. Almost everyone knew about the problem, but they assumed it was someone else's responsibility. The Plant Manager (who was, in fact, unaware of the situation) usually got the blame. "He must know about this, so it must be OK. Therefore it's hands off for everyone else."

When the group understood how much each of them had contributed to the development of this harmful pattern, they began to get depressed. The facilitator quickly moved them on by asking, "How *should* maintenance be handled? We're pretty clear about what we don't want: How do we want it to be?"

Obviously, Maintenance needed to reclaim its responsibility and insist on regularly scheduled preventive maintenance. In general, they needed to be much more assertive about their role. While the supervisors needed the right to occasionally plead special exceptions, everyone had to assume responsibility for asking, "Is this a new policy or an exception?" By staying clear on the goal—a smoothly functioning and productive plant—it was easy to see that everyone bore responsibility for achieving that goal.

Conclusion

All of us learn all the time. We often divide experiences into either failures or new possibilities. The choice generates subtle, powerful differences. The first attitude keeps narrowing the list of possible ways to reach your goal; the second broadens the possibilities. The first attitude fundamentally assumes disempowerment and naturally leads to shifting responsibility elsewhere. By paying attention to the frame you are in, you have more choice about the results you get than at any point further on. Once you enter the Aim Frame, you are moving forward and leading others forward as well. The next step is to make your chosen goals clear, complete, and compelling.

CHAPTER FIVE

Starting Point: What You and Your Customers Want

"Wait a minute! You are talking to *engineers* here! Techies! Professionals! What can you tell *us* about setting goals and planning? We wrote the books on those processes."

We gladly concede your expertise at making goals detailed and explicit. Most technical and professional disciplines have developed important tools and techniques for designing work flow, measurement, diagnosis, and so forth. However, an aspect of the planning process that still needs improvement is the tendency to plan thoroughly for end results other than the ones that are needed or wanted. What is missing is a simple, underlying structure to goal-setting that allows you to focus on the bigger picture as well as the details.

Purpose

We continue working within the Syntax Model, exploring the PLAN facet. Like the previous chapter, this is hands-on: You actually get to *do* something. It is an opportunity to understand what it takes to achieve compelling goals and to practice designing them. We introduce you to a powerful and easy-to-use format for developing goals to which you can apply your tools and techniques with increased likelihood of success.

Getting the Big Picture

Let's start with rework. "Well, why didn't they say they wanted *that?*" you mutter on the way back to the drawing board for the umpteenth time. Stop! Before you re-plan or re-design this time, back up a minute and see if instead of repeating the same mistakes in a more thorough fashion, you can approach the situation a little differently.

In reality, there is one reason for doing work: Somebody wants it done. The work you do helps people get what they want or need. Whenever you incorrectly interpret what they want or need, there will be undesirable consequences—which may mean that you get less of what *you* want or need.

By understanding that you need to construct an accurate mental model with the person with the need, and by eliciting what they actually want rather than what you think he or she *should* want or what *you* would want in their position, you can cut to the core of the work and ensure its completion. This is the central purpose of mutual understanding.

Without this piece in place, we may solve the wrong problem or only part of the right problem. Plans never get implemented because they do not match reality. Or, by the time they are implemented, they are so far behind schedule, or circumstances have changed so much that it no longer matters.

Here is a tool for locating hidden data and embedded assumptions *before* you start to work on a task.

Elements of Good Goals: Direction, Motivation, and Evidence

By using certain procedures for developing goals, you will understand what the other person wants. You can also balance it with a clear idea of what you want. (You won't have a great work life if you continually undermine, give up, or are unclear about what *you* want.) The broad questions that delineate the big picture should be answered both for you and for the person or group requesting work.

Effective goal-setting includes three components: direction, motivation, and evidence of accomplishment. In practice, those are the answers to these simple questions (see Figure 5-1):

1. What do I want?
2. What will that get me?
3. How will I know when I have it?

Direction	What do you/we want?
Motivation	What will that get you/us?
Evidence	How will we know when we get there?

FIGURE 5-1: QUESTIONS FOR EFFECTIVE GOALS

Like a lot of seemingly simple things, the power is in the details. For example, when a large automotive company learned that its customers were dissatisfied with its warranties, it reduced the price of the warranties. The company wasted a lot of time and money before bothering to ask the questions that located the real source of the dissatisfaction: not the warranty's price, but the number of trips to the dealer that the warranties required customers to make. A little more time clarifying what customers *really* wanted could have saved untold frustration and dollars. We call it "go slow to go fast."

Creating a Goal for Yourself

We invite you now to try it out. Our goal is for you, the reader, to understand at a personal level how developing a goal thoroughly leads to achieving it. Grab a sheet of paper or open a computer file. Write down a personal goal you would like to achieve in three months. Pick something work-related (a promotion) or home-related (painting a room) or personal (exercising three times a week or spending more quality time with your family). Stay in the near-term for the purpose of this exercise, although the technique works for the long-term as well. Keep the *direction* goal statement brief—a sentence or two. For example: "I want to get the project proposal completed and out the door."

Next, write down your answer to the *motivation* question: "What will that get me?" Then ask: "What will reaching *that* goal get me?" Then ask it again: "What will *that* get me?" Keep asking until you get the same answer three times in a row. Then you know you have hit bedrock. Hitting bedrock is critical. Otherwise, you do not build in the true motivators. You may end up believing, for instance, that your goal is to get rich when it really is to have the time to do the things you love.

Did you find out anything interesting? Any significant shifts in emphasis? Any useful information about where your bigger priorities lie? Or where your heart is leading? Based on what you learned, write a revised goal statement, one that incorporates what you now know about what you want.

Your proposed goal might, for example, evolve from "I want to get the project proposal written and out the door," to "I want to get the project proposal completed and out the door so that Gerry starts to notice my work," to, finally, "I want to get the project proposal written and out the door so that Gerry starts to believe I'm capable of bigger things and I get to work on more exciting and rewarding projects." Once you understand that the real goal is to work on more exciting and rewarding projects, you can figure out whether getting the proposal out the door is the best path to that end. Let's assume it is and continue.

Now you might think you are done with your goal statement, but you are not. You still have not answered the "truth-serum" question: "How will I know when I have reached it?" "Oh yeah, 'measurable indicators of success.' I know how to do that," is what you may be thinking. Well, yes and no. *Evidence is* measurable indicators, but with more detail and precision than ever before.

Having Your Goal Before You Have It

The next set of steps creates a three-dimensional depiction of having achieved the goal. Reality is a composite of all the information our senses gather: We need all the data in order to know if our goal works or not. Subsequent chapters will discuss *how* our senses gather that information and what our minds do with it. For the moment, the key point is that goals that work are goals that include information about what our primary sensing systems—hearing (auditory), seeing (visual) and feeling (kinesthetic)—will experience. Full representations of goals have power and momentum; they are alive inside our minds. By extending from what is to what could be, they draw us forward.

Let's work on building your goal this way. The first time, see it through your own eyes as the one having the experience. Let's go:

> *What specifically will you **see** that indicates you have accomplished your goal? The smiling faces of your teammates? Flip charts detailing a successful process flow? The clear blue of a summer sky as you drift across the lake? Write it down.*

> *What will you **hear**? It might be the sound of a smoothly humming machine, or someone congratulating you, or you saying, "By George, I think I've got it!" Write that down. What are you saying to yourself? "This is really working!" "Boy, does this feel great!" "Yes!!!" "Damn, I'm good!" Include those notes.*

> *What will you **feel**? The heft of a perfectly machined widget? The comfort of leaning back in your chair with your feet up on the desk? The satisfaction of seamless software that works? The pleasure of a job well done? Or the rush of adrenaline as the whole team cheers? Add these ideas to your notes.*

The point is to capture as much detail as you can about *how you will know* you have accomplished your goal. And to notice which sense you have to stretch for. That is often the sensory description that enriches your goal the most, even though (or maybe because) you are least conscious of it. For example, if it is easy to see what you will see and hear what you will hear but difficult to feel what you will feel, then there is a good chance that seeing it and hearing it alone will not make you know you accomplished it. When you know what you will feel and recognize having those feelings at the time, *then* it becomes real. You *know* you have done it!

Let's sharpen the detail level with a second iteration, this time from an outside observer's point of view. It is three months from now and you have achieved the goal developed in this chapter. Where will you be *at the exact moment* you know you have achieved it? Be there now. Picture that setting and add any details you now notice: the color of the walls or sky, the furniture or the trees and bushes, the pictures on the wall, the view from the window, or whatever else makes that location specific and vivid.

Who else is with you? What are they wearing? What are the expressions on their faces? Include anything else that is significant; the final report with a spiffy cover, your backpack leaning next to a tree, the car you have restored gleaming in the garage, or the color and layout of the paycheck in your hand bearing higher numbers than ever before.

Listen for a moment. What do you hear at the moment you know you have achieved your goal? Is it the sound of the wind rushing through the pines, or your boss congratulating you on an outstanding job, or the cheer of the crowd as you cross the finish line, or the quietly humming vibration of a well-tuned machine? Make a note, and make it as detailed as you can. Note voice tones and tempos.

Next, observe yourself at the moment of achievement. How are you standing or sitting? What are you wearing, and how do those clothes feel? How are you breathing? Write it down. What is your facial expression; serene, exultant, content, exhilarated, peaceful, exuberant? Whatever it is, write it down.

By now you have a good deal of detail about the point at which you know you have achieved your goal. Here is how you find out if the detail is sufficient: Describe your goal to someone else and how you will know when you have reached it. Ask your helper to listen with this filter: If they walked in at the moment when you know you have reached your goal, could they tell, without asking, that you have done it? If not, ask them to help you elicit more detail. *Do not*, repeat, *do not* start to think about *how* to reach that goal. Just get the details of the moment of recognition into your mind.

Future Check

Now ask one more favor of your helper. Remember the old Chinese curse, "May you get what you asked for"? We have all had the experience of wanting something, getting it, and finding out it was not really what we wanted.

Here is a way to *have* the future for a moment, in order to double check that it is what you really want and, if necessary, fine tune it. Have your helper say the following:

"It is now three months in the future. You have reached your goal. Be there now.

"See (and fill in with the details you have given them).

"Hear (and they fill in from your details). Say (and they fill in) to yourself.

"Feel (they describe your physical and emotional states).

"Now check: is this exactly what you want? Is anything missing?"

Take time to scan the holographic representation of your wishes. Be there. See it, hear it, feel it, smell it, and taste it if you can. Is it *precisely* the way you want it to be? Is everyone and everything there that should be there? Make notes on anything you discover from asking these questions.

One interesting benefit of the last step is to reveal things that turn out to have strategic importance when we plan to actually achieve our goal. For example, "Ed and Marty were not in the room when we were drinking the toast. They should have been there." Later you can figure out at what point Ed and Marty need to get involved to be there for that ultimate moment. Good thing you noticed it now!

What *They* Want: The Basis for Getting All Work Done

"Well, this is nice for personal goals, but I certainly couldn't use it at work!" This may be running through your mind about now. What exactly is stopping you? "It's too *soft*—too *weird*." Is it? Or is it just too demanding and precise? Remember, setting good goals for yourself is only half the battle. If you do not learn how to set quality goals with the people you work with—in pairs or on teams or with customers—your effectiveness will be profoundly limited. When everyone pictures the same end result, they can make their best contribution.

Shared Goals for Projects

Let's play with the idea for a few minutes. You are a consulting engineer for a large automotive supplier. The customer wants a new electrical housing or junction box for the computers that run the newest model engines. Of course, they have a brand new whiz kid who knows computers inside out and backwards but knows nothing about getting them to work in the hostile environment of a modern automobile engine compartment. You receive his specs via E-mail. You study them, get a handle on the problem (you think), and start to design the prototype.

"So where are the openings for the other three circuits for the A/C system?" the customer coolly inquires when you meet to review the prototype design.

"So where were they on your specs?" you mutter as you return to your work station.

On the second try he says, "Looks all right, let's build a prototype." You send the drawings to the prototype shop. In the process, neither of you has noticed that the site for the final product rests directly above the cam shaft, one of the hottest parts of the engine. Thus, neither of you notices that the material specified "cannot be used in environments exceeding 500 degrees Fahrenheit" when the prototype comes back.

Had someone bothered to check for direction, motivation, and evidence, the outcome could have been quite different. Contrast the preceding with this: When the young wizard comes to you initially, you say, "Can we take a few minutes to review these specs?"

He says, "Listen, I'm busy. It's all in there. I haven't got time for this!"

Then you say, "I've learned the hard way it's worth taking a little time on the front end of these kinds of requests in order to save a lot of time and expense at the other end. Please bear with me. First, tell me what you need."

Whiz: "A housing for the electrical circuitry that supports the fourteen additional computers going into the new models. Just like it says there on the first page."

You: "And what exactly would this housing for the electrical circuitry get you?"

Whiz: "It would get us a safe environment, one that protects these computers. A couple of them are going to be pretty critical for maintaining the new safety standards."

You: "Can you tell me what you mean when you say 'safe environment'?"

Whiz: "Well, these little babies can't get wet, and they can't get too hot, and obviously you don't want anything corrosive near them."

You: "Great, this is very helpful. Tell me more about 'too hot.'"

Whiz: "If they get in environments over 300 degrees they won't run."

You: "Three hundred degrees! That's a significant design constraint. Now, let's assume we've got the safe environment for these fourteen new computers. What else would this new housing get you?"

Whiz: "It would get us an easy way for the mechanics to run diagnostics on the new systems these computers will be running."

You: "Ah, the housing has to offer an easy way to run diagnostics. That's real important. Anything else?"

Whiz: "Not that I can think of."

You: "OK, we'll assume for the moment that you've got housing that provides a computer-safe environment and easy diagnostics. What would having *that* get you?"

He: "My team has over fifteen months invested in developing the circuitry and programming for these new systems. It would protect and complete our effort."

You: "So it has to protect your investments?"

Whiz: "Yeah, and then it allows us to finally field test our software designs. We think we've pioneered some pretty exciting new stuff, but we won't know until we actually install and see them run. If our designs are as good as we think, this will be a career high for everyone on the team. We're pretty sure Marketing can build a whole new campaign around what these babies can do—the customers will love it!"

You: "Let me make sure I've got it all now. Having a housing that provides a computer-safe environment and easy diagnostics will protect your team's fifteen-month investment in developing new software designs and allow you to finally field test your work. If it's successful, customer satisfaction levels will skyrocket, you'll have a whole new way to sell cars, and your team will be golden. Did I leave anything out?"

Whiz: "Well, I hadn't thought about it like that before, but it sounds great! I never realized that getting this housing designed right was such a big deal!"

You: "Neither did I until we took a little extra time to explore it. Will you hang with me for one final data check? I want to make sure we both know exactly how we'll know we've achieved the goal."

Whiz: "What more is there to do? Seems pretty clear to me now."

You: "You're probably right, but I'd like to be doubly sure. We'd hate to slow this process down when you guys are so close to the finish line."

Whiz: "Oh, all right. What do I have to do?"

You: "Well, imagine we've built the housing, and you're holding it in your hands. Tell me exactly what you see."

Whiz: "What I see? This seems pretty silly, but OK. I see a black injection molded plastic form, about two inches by three inches, with four openings for the plugs for the diagnostics, one for the battery connection, and three for the cables to the safety system, cooling system, and the wipers."

You: "Good. Anything else you see about the housing?"

Whiz: "Well, one side is flat so that it can fit alongside the vacuum actuator."

You: "Ah. Any particular reason for placing it there?"

Whiz: "Just that it would make it easier to reach for diagnostics."

You: "OK. Easy diagnostics is the goal. Anything else you see?"

Whiz: "I don't think so. I've got the dimensions on the openings all written up for you here."

You: "Great, thanks! Now tell me what you feel when you're holding the housing."

Whiz: "Feel? I don't feel anything. What do you mean, 'feel'?"

You: "What does it weigh? Is it rough or smooth? Does it have sharp edges? Stuff like that."

Whiz: "Oh, I thought you meant was I happy or something."

You: "Well, we'll get to that in a minute. Now just tell me about the physical aspects of it."

Whiz: "OK. It's heavy because it has to provide so much protection; it's smooth, no rough edges; each of the openings sticks out about one-half inch and tapers so that it's an exact fit with the cable. No room for garbage to get inside."

You: "Several very useful items there. Anything else?"

Whiz: "Naw, can't think of anything."

You: "OK, let's assume for a moment that the one you were holding in your hand is now installed. Is there anything you'd hear that would tell you things were running smoothly?"

Whiz: "It's more like what you wouldn't hear. Part of our new design is a significant sound reduction associated with these new systems, both under the hood and inside the car."

You: "Excellent. Assuming that's true, what would your team be saying to each other? What might you be saying to yourself?"

Whiz: "Well, we'd all start cheering when we realized how quietly the engine was running, and we'd do high fives, and clap. I'd be saying 'Man, it doesn't get any better than this!'"

You: "And what would your emotional state be at that point?"

Whiz: "Well, I'd be flying 'cause, you know, it's not often you get a success like that. I'd feel pretty darn good."

You: "Perfect! Now let me wrap this up. Imagine it's six months from now and you've just finished a successful field test. Be there for a moment. The housing worked, the computers worked, the new systems worked, the car is running quietly and more safely than any car ever has. The whole team is there, cheering, doing high fives, and clapping. The hood is up and you can see the black housing sitting right where you'd pictured it, seven projections sticking out in just the right places with all the cables fitting perfectly and going exactly where they should go. You're really flying, saying to yourself, 'Man, it doesn't get any better than this!' Really get into that moment, have that experience. Got it?"

Whiz: "Yeah, I guess so."

You: "OK, now check: Is this *exactly* what you want? Look around, listen, feel it. Is anything missing?"

Whiz: "Well, now that you mention it, I am realizing something. There's no wiring for the indicator light to the dashboard. There's supposed to be an indicator light on the dash to warn if any of these systems is getting ready to fail. It's part of the customer-satisfaction element. We completely forgot to specify it in our designs. Wow! That would have meant big-time trouble if we hadn't caught it in time. Other than that, though, I think things are just perfect."

You: "All right! Thanks for sticking with me. I think we got a lot of useful information through this process."

Shared Goals for Teams

Every human experience has three sensory components; visual, auditory, and kinesthetic. The more details you articulate, the more powerful your visions. These visions allow people to buy in, become a part of, and fully support the goals. Information about what you want is almost always buried somewhere in your mind; accessing it often requires effort. Surfacing those details is akin to creating an internal hologram, a three-dimensional verification of your assumptions.

It is tempting to stop at that point. "It's perfectly clear inside my head, why can't you see it?" This is the implicit reason for millions of misunderstandings every day. The discipline of verbalizing a goal has several benefits:

- It can provide key bits of information which will subsequently need strategic attention (for example, "When do we bring Ed and Marty on board?");
- It allows us to confirm the desirability of the goal, or adjust it to maximize desirability;
- It forces us to verbalize what is obvious to us but not necessarily to others;
- It forms the basis for creating *mutual understanding* about reaching that goal.

The last point is significant. Effective leaders have in common an ability to "create worlds to which others want to belong."[1] Leaders articulate—and demonstrate by their behavior—the goals so precisely, so vividly, so acutely that the goals become alive. Their visions and goals become compelling. Others can see, hear, and feel what reaching those goals will be like, so they want to—and feel invited to—join in. With the shared understanding the leader has generated, others can also move closer to the goal.

You may be thinking, "I don't recall having signed on for leadership of anything. I'm not interested in leadership. I'm interested in getting the job done." Exactly. And getting the job done in the New Workplace means taking your turn as leader. Leadership today has become everyone's responsibility. Work is too complex and too demanding to put all that pressure on just one person.

Simple questions about direction, motivation, and evidence are a great starting point. As you experiment with asking these questions, notice how oth-

---

[1] Robert Dilts and G. Bonissone, *Skills for the Future* (Capitola, California: Meta Publications, 1993).

ers respond more positively, how they get more excited about and supportive of your goals, especially when you articulate them with details in all
three representational systems.

The process is especially useful for teams about to embark on major new
projects. Specifying an outcome up front allows team members to make the
right decisions all along the way, decisions that accurately and efficiently
facilitate those outcomes. It minimizes needless power struggles that stem
from different ideas of the goal. As an added benefit, delineating the goal
lets you check it out from multiple points of view: How does it look, sound,
and feel to the customer or end-user? To Management? To Engineering? To
Marketing?

Notice again: The power is in the details. You know that about your work.
It is equally true about the communication process. Many people think rough
approximations will do. Effective communicators know—or have learned
the hard way—that precise language and plenty of details increase their
success rate. Seeing the big picture in detail gives you the flexibility to alter
responses when you recognize whether they move you toward or away
from your goals.

Consumer Protection Warning: Goals are not static. Revisit them regularly,
both to breathe new life into them and to adjust them to current conditions,
changes in personnel, customer needs, market trends, and so forth. The
goal must evolve along with the person or group—even as it provides the
core principles around which the person or group operates. Effective individuals and teams instinctively know that continual adaptation is a part of
managing shared work.

Conclusion

We all carry a rich data base about our goals in our heads. As these detailed
examples make clear, we know what we want, albeit not always consciously.
Shared understanding of purpose and possibility is a powerful motivator. In
the New Workplace Game, taking the time to delineate *direction, motivation* and *evidence* lets the team evolve its understanding of what is possible. At the same time, each member makes a contribution. Through systematic inquiry and communication, we can arrive at a mutual understanding
that improves the quality of results as well as the quality of teamwork.

CHAPTER SIX

Are You Ready and Willing to Listen?

Now your goals are clear. Given your background and preferences as a professional, what else do you need to work effectively under the new guidelines? The next step is to shift your attention away from work itself and onto the process by which work gets done—the interpersonal process. If you have spent your whole life focused on work issues, learning to notice how other people respond to you, to the situation, or to other people is a major step.

Purpose

This chapter addresses the act of listening. The dictionary defines listening as "paying attention to sound, hearing with thoughtful attention."[1] We want to expand that definition because effective listening means paying attention with *all* of our senses. There is more to listening than just sound. Research by Albert Mehrabian at UCLA indicates that 7 percent of our message is conveyed through our word choices, 38 percent by our voice, and 55 percent by whether we appear congruent with our message.[2]

Much of that perception of congruence is based on the level of rapport between the speaker and the listener. Chapter Six covers attitudes and methods for building rapport effectively in the New Workplace. This is the first of two chapters in the LINK section of the Model of Effectiveness.

Tools, Not Rules

We are not addressing content issues as we enter this discussion of rapport; we have switched to context. There are no specific rules with guaranteed results. Effective behavior is *always* context-specific. What works in one

---

[1] *Webster's Seventh New Collegiate Dictionary* (Springfield, Mass.: G.& C. Merriam Co., 1969) 493.

[2] Albert Mehrabian, *Silent Messages* (Belmont, California: Wadsworth, 1971).

situation may bomb in another. It is *your* job to pay enough attention to adjust your behavior in response to the context. This is one of the differences between amateur and professional communicators. Amateurs ignore everything but *their* interests, *their* subject, *their* desires, and whine when they do not get the results they want. Professionals pay attention to themselves, to other people, to the situation, and they keep trying new actions until they get their desired results. They never lose sight of mutual understanding.

Professional communicators understand that *the meaning of your communication is the response you get*. Read that sentence slowly and carefully—it is one of the most important ideas in this book. It means you may no longer blame others when communication goes awry. You can't think, "He's a jerk," or "She wasn't listening," or "They really didn't want to hear what I had to say." Instead, you must think, "Hmmm, that didn't work. What could I do differently next time to get the results I want?" It is easy to blame others for not listening; it is harder to find ways to communicate that encourage people to listen. Yet the demands of the New Game require you to develop the flexibility to do just that.

As a professional communicator, you measure the meaning—the effect—of communication by the responses you receive. You understand that what is *intended* to be communicated is often not the same as what is *actually* communicated. When communication is successful and mutual understanding is established, the resulting actions are what were planned or desired. When people do not communicate successfully, the results are not what is wanted. The results are indicative, however, of what *was* communicated rather than what was *intended*. To measure the effectiveness of your communication, use actual results as feedback.

There are times when people really *are* jerks or don't listen or do not appreciate the value of what you have to offer. However, the excuse is used far more often than reality may warrant. Even if people are acting like jerks, we cannot change them, but we *can* change our own behavior. Most of the time, human beings communicate sloppily and are surprised at the sloppy results they get. When we set out to achieve understanding and bring more precision into the communication process, we experience remarkable improvement—in everyday life as well as in our work.

Bad News and Good News

The bad news is that you lose the right to blame others when things do not work. The good news is that when you realize that your behavior (the words you choose as well as the non-verbal messages that accompany those words) has direct impact on the outcome, you realize that you have far more power than you thought.

This recognition can be remarkably liberating. You have probably heard the word "empowerment" recently. *Professional communication skills are central to real empowerment.* When *you* choose your responses instead of just reacting, you gain control. Having control over what is happening in your life looks, sounds, and feels better than being life's victim!

Consider this example: During the course of a large reorganization, a technical supervisor loses his position and is assigned to a team. At first, he is angry and bitter. He notices, however, that the other members of the team are all quite senior people with whom he would not ordinarily get to work. He also recognizes that the nature of his new responsibilities are in scope and responsibility far above his last assignment. "Whether or not they meant it that way, this really is quite an opportunity," he thinks. He decides not to let his initial disappointment prevent him from doing some of the best, most satisfying work of his career. As a result, he is able to shift his attention to the goal and to the other team members' concerns, and creates an excellent first impression.

Behavior as the Data Source

Human experience has three parts: feelings, thoughts, and behavior. Of the three, only someone else's *behavior* is accessible to you. Only behavior can be seen, felt, heard—apprehended by your senses. Similarly, what *you* think or feel can only be inferred from your behavior. Remember when someone told you they were thinking "x" when it was clear from their behavior that they were really thinking "y"? This distinction between what we think we think and what we really believe and practice is what Argyris calls "espoused theory vs. theory-in-use."[3] We are all incongruent sometimes. Truly effective people minimize this; they "walk their talk."

This is one reason paying attention to others is so important. Professional communicators understand that their interpretations of other people's behavior influences their internal processes and hence their own behavior. They use other people's behavior as information. They also understand that their own behavior, including their words, provides information to others. They know that if they change that behavior, they can influence the outcome.

---

[3] Chris Argyris, *Knowledge for Action* (San Francisco: Jossey-Bass, 1993).

Listening: The Magic in Communication

Listening involves paying attention not only to words, but to non-verbal communication as well. Done well, this kind of listening is the magic essence of *attention* which allows for mutual understanding and opens a pathway to trust and teamwork. Attending only to words and ignoring other data sabotages the communication process.

How do others know you are listening? They perceive your behavior. Your behavior demonstrates your responsiveness. Try this experiment: Listen to someone's words so closely that you can repeat them verbatim. While doing this, maintain a neutral body posture and voice tone. As you hear each word, note your own reaction. Would the other person experience you as "listening"?

What people call a "good listener" is actually someone good at establishing rapport. This can be done so thoroughly that the flow of communication becomes virtually seamless. You link up in an atmosphere of respect and trust that enhances mutual understanding and ability to perform well.

What Is Rapport?

Rapport means being "in tune" with someone else, on his or her wave length. Rapport creates the conditions under which efficient and effective communication can occur. Indeed, we have little influence with others *unless* we establish rapport with them.

Do you easily establish rapport with some colleagues, but feel mismatched with others? Rapport stems from meeting others "where they are." In doing so, you offer a behavioral statement of respect and illustrate your willingness to interact. When you have plenty in common, such as background, interests, or temperament, this occurs naturally.

Those who are extraordinarily effective have the capacity to establish rapport with a vast range of people. They have the gift of finding something in common with almost everyone, even if there are no gender, cultural, professional, or class affinities. This does not mean they give up their own identities, but they are flexible enough to facilitate communication under almost any circumstances.

To achieve your personal and professional goals in the New Workplace, the ability to establish rapport with a wide range of people is a *very* useful skill. Contrary to what you may believe, this is a skill that can be learned, developed, and improved. This doesn't mean becoming phony or insincere, but it does mean indulging your innate curiosity. When people fascinate you as much as technical or professional issues do, you create a powerful systems dynamic. Think about how you respond to someone who obviously finds you interesting. That's how other people respond when you clearly find them interesting.

The Issue of Manipulation

People who deliberately attempt to establish rapport send non-verbal messages of acceptance and interest. People also choose words that tell the other person "I am like you and use similar words for similar thoughts."

These conscious behaviors raise the question of manipulation. Am I manipulating you by focusing my attention on you and adjusting my behavior to mirror yours? If I attempt to influence you by leading you toward my goal without being heavy-handed or obvious, am I taking a controlling position in the communication?

This is an important question because it has as much to do with whether it is OK to be conscious about your behavior as it does with manipulating others. People with greater awareness of the communication process and more choices in communication behavior have more influence on the outcome of communication.

People with "street smarts" have heightened awareness, gained by paying close attention to details of behavior. They have a repertoire of responses available to match the other person. The "smarts" part is that their actions produce certain outcomes. However, if you ask them how they do it, it is unlikely that they can tell you. Our research indicates that even if they think they know what they are doing, they probably are wrong. What makes them effective is not what they think it is!

"Manipulation" has certain negative implications—that someone is taking unfair advantage of someone else; that it is one person doing something to the other, rather than an exchange; and that one person's consciousness of what he or she is doing controls the other person. When people mention manipulation, the underlying concern is "What are your *intentions* toward me? Do you wish to do me harm or benefit yourself at my expense?"

We believe that using principles of effective communication actually reduces the negative, exploitative element of manipulation. There are three reasons for this. First, the ideal is to offer communication tools to as many people as possible. The tools are openly available, and they are based on observable principles. Second, when people are conscious of linking with others, they are better at attending to the other person and synchronizing goals. Third, while people can become better communicators, they still cannot assert control unless the other person participates. Communication is a system, and each of us elects to participate in that system in our own way.

Communication skills are not the oppressive tool of the manipulator. They are demystifying and exchanging tools. If you are concerned about manipulating someone when you are conscious of your communication, ask yourself what you are concerned about. Perhaps you have questions about whether you have goals in common, or whether you are working to mutual benefit. Once you have figured this out, you can discuss it with the other person. The result is usually better collaboration.

Consumer Protection Warning: When you act as if you find someone interesting, it is nearly impossible not to find them so. Further, it is very difficult to establish rapport with people and not end up liking them. Therefore, we do not believe the expansion of rapport-building skills makes you manipulative. If you care about the people with whom you have rapport, you are less likely to manipulate them for selfish ends.

Behavioral Matching— Posture and Gestures

The three types of basic nonverbal behaviors for establishing rapport include: **matching behavior, matching voice tone and tempo,** and **matching moods and emotional states.**

To understand behavioral matching, recall the last time you were around a couple who had just fallen in love. How often did their postures and gestures mirror each other?

This tendency to mirror may be pre-programmed. Research at Brown University on mother-child reciprocity confirms that infants are born with a repertoire of actions that encourage their mothers to bond with them, even as they are bonding to their mothers or other significant caregivers. High-quality attachment results in improved neurological development.[4] Another study shows that mothers and infants who sleep together mirror each other's breathing patterns, even when sound asleep.[5] In our workshops, most people have difficulty breaking rapport with each other, even when asked to do so in a demonstration activity.

---

[4] *The Brown University Child and Adolescent Behavior Letter,* October 1991, 8.

[5] J.J. McKenna, "An Anthropological Perspective on the Sudden Infant Death Syndrome (SIDS): The Role of Prenatal Breathing Cues and Speech Breathing Adaptations," *Medical Anthropology 10,* (1986) 8–92.

At the same time, we often break rapport inadvertently—the phone rings, someone comes into our office, we remember a meeting we skipped—and the results can be devastating. The stronger the rapport, the more desperately others will seek to regain it. They become more animated, match body language, lean forward to make eye contact or ask questions to draw us back when we break rapport. If the person is thrown off enough, he or she will give up entirely and withdraw from the communication.

Matching Physical Behavior

Assuming a similar posture is the most obvious example of behavioral matching. It has many practical applications. For instance, at a meeting with the company president, you notice that he is sitting erect and "formal" in his chair. You do not assume a relaxed posture until the president does. Many of our trainees were initially skeptical about the efficacy of this idea until they tried it.

One corporate employee, Curtis, tells of meeting the new division president during yet another company reorganization. The president was coming for a site tour, and as the "low man" on the corporate organizational chart, Curtis was assigned to go along. Bored, he decided to experiment with matching the new president's body language and gestures. By the end of the tour, the president was addressing all his answers to him, no matter who had asked the question.

On the way back to the company cafeteria for lunch, the president ignored all the highly-placed executives and started talking to Curtis as though they were old friends. They chatted comfortably all through lunch. Afterwards, the other executives asked Curtis if he and the new president were old friends. "No, I'd never laid eyes on the guy before today." Needless to say, he is now a great believer in non-verbal matching.

Posture and gestures are obvious candidates for non-verbal matching. This does not mean aping or mimicking people, but it does mean being in sync with their natural rhythms and patterns. Their legs may be crossed at the knee and yours at the ankle. They may be tapping a foot while you tap a pencil. They may talk with their hands while you talk with your shoulders. The patterns and rhythms still match.

As you begin to pay attention to other people's behavior in order to match it, you will notice some of the many "micromoves" we make when communicating. Head tilt, eye-blink rate, subtle changes in skin color across the cheeks and upper throat area, changes in the size and configuration of the lips, tightening or relaxing of the muscles around the lips and eyes, tightening of the muscles at the back of the jaw or in the throat, dilation or expansion of pupil size, breathing rate and location, eye movements—we have myriad ways to telegraph what is going on inside of us.

Similarly, micromoves have auditory and kinesthetic complements: tightened throat muscles constrict the vocal chords; shifts in breathing location from the abdomen to the upper chest affect resonance; shifts in timbre or intonation communicate changes in feeling states. Timing, tone, pauses, speed, all convey messages beyond the words themselves.

You may be thinking, "Yeah, but I never notice any of that stuff. I'm too busy paying attention to the conversation itself." Yes and no. Consciously, you may not notice. Unconsciously, however, your brain is capturing all that detail. The eyes alone map to twelve different areas of the brain, according to current research.[6] Each area develops an incredibly detailed rendering of what the eye records. Much of what we attribute to "intuition" or "hunches" is undoubtedly our unconscious feeding us a compilation of the data it collects.

Matching Voice Tone and Tempo

Apart from matching words and ways of representing experience, we use the voice to build rapport. Matching tone and tempo may be more common than you think. In phone conversations, have you ever started echoing the regional accent of the person on the other end of the line? Likewise, you may unconsciously mimic the distinctly rhythmic patterns of someone who speaks British, Scottish, Irish, Australian, East Indian, or West Indian English. Becoming aware of this matching may embarrass you. Rarely, however, will the person on the receiving end notice the shift in your speech pattern. Instead, they will just think you have become friendlier and more likable. *People like people who seem like them.*

In stressful situations, vocal matching can be a particularly effective tool. Erica, a Syntax consultant, tells of her experience during a long transatlantic flight:

"On one of my flights home to Europe to deliver training, I was reading a book. Suddenly I heard loud voices and saw a young woman walking back and forth screaming in Spanish, 'Where are my children? Where are my children?' Two flight attendants were following her and trying to calm her down. Of course, they kept trying to talk her out of her behavior. She reached for the intercom phone so that every passenger could hear this pathetic message: 'I want to get off this plane! I want to leave the plane!' It was clear that she was out of touch with reality. Her children were not on board, and she certainly was not able to leave the plane at 35,000 feet!

---

[6] Geoffrey Montgomery, "The Mind's Eye," *Discovery*, May 1991, 51.

"Next, she ran to the emergency exit door. Can you imagine the panicked faces on the passengers at that moment? At that instant, I stood up and ran to her. I put my hands on her shoulders and started to scream with her in the same tone, pitch, and words. Of course, the other people stared, thinking that now they had two crazy women!

"When I gained rapport with her by matching her behavior, meaning 'I understand you,' my next move was to lead. I gradually slowed my tempo and lowered my voice until she calmed down enough to be managed by the flight attendants. That day I really appreciated my training in communication!"

By meeting the young woman where she was—matching language, voice tone, volume, and tempo—Erica was able to build enough rapport so that when she calmed her voice down, the woman was able to do the same. In this case, being soothing and calm, as flight attendants are traditionally taught, created a mismatch that prevented them from reaching through the young woman's distress.

Did you ever struggle to stay calm and rational when someone else was angry and upset, and later found out that they perceived *you* as hostile and controlling? Meeting people where they are means acknowledging their emotional state. While professionals place high value on rational discourse, they get upset, frustrated, hurt, or angry just like everyone else. If it feels risky to acknowledge those feelings directly, do it indirectly by matching voice tone, pitch, and tempo. You are letting the other person know he or she has been heard.

Matching Mental and Emotional States

Has someone ever barged into your office for a little relaxing gossip just when you had finally focused on an important project? Or has someone ever bounced in cheerfully and started chattering when you were in a foul humor and wanted to be left alone? Obviously, these folks didn't remember, or didn't know, about matching, in this case matching your mood. Had they taken the trouble to notice your mood at that moment, they might have changed their approach and had a more productive encounter.

Other forms of matching include recognizing others' views of life and the world. This commonly occurs during conversations about the weather, sports, and politics. Sharing common experiences—growing up in the same town, going to the same college, belonging to the same fraternity or sorority, having the same number of children—are traditional forms of matching. So are noticing similar ethnic, cultural, and religious backgrounds. Today, it is increasingly important to match universal human feelings and experiences to cross barriers of background or culture.

Once Eleanor Roosevelt had a visitor in the White House who was rather nervous to begin with. The guest became more tense after she knocked a precious teacup off the table and it smashed into pieces. A short while later, Mrs. Roosevelt elbowed another cup onto the floor, an act of matching that was the only way she could have relieved the guest's embarrassment. Here was a truly professional communicator at work!

When all else fails, remembering and commenting on a shared goal can create the rapport that is the object of matching.

Taking the Lead

After determining that you have established rapport, move the conversation toward your goals (that is, "take the lead"). Figure 6-1 diagrams what happens during conversations when one person takes the lead. Before you take the lead, determine your goals and pay attention to the other person. Once you establish rapport, move the conversation towards your goal—gathering information, figuring out how to get the job done, developing new ideas, or whatever else it might be.

Whether the move is gradual or direct will depend on your assessment of the situation, including the level of rapport and the other person's timing. For example, some people like to get right down to the business at hand. Others prefer to move more deliberately. Neither is right nor wrong—they are just different and it is your job to notice and adjust. Otherwise you can quickly undo all you have done to build rapport.

Listening to Move Toward Your Goals

If you are unsure of the rapport, try a "trial lead." This is usually a nonverbal lead, such as shifting posture and then waiting a bit. If the other person shifts into a similar position, the trial lead has been accepted, and you can now offer a verbal lead. If either lead is rejected, immediately return to matching until better rapport is established: This is a case where persistence will *not* pay off.

Establishing and maintaining rapport is not a linear process. Frequently, you will cycle the loop several times before reaching your goal. The hardest part is knowing when to shift attention. As long as the conversation is moving steadily and work is being accomplished, stay focused on what you are discussing. At the slightest indication that things are slowing down or that rapport is weakening, shift your attention.

"Yes, but if my attention is focused on the content, how will I notice those 'indications'?" Good question. Part of the trick is to increase the signal value

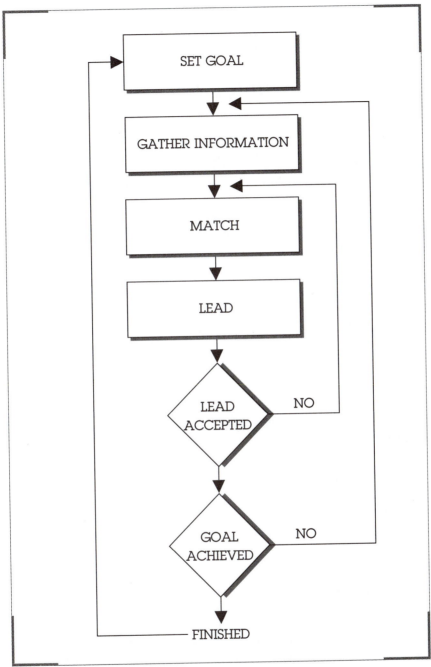

FIGURE 6-1: ESTABLISHING RAPPORT AND LEADING TOWARD GOALS[7]

---

[7] Flow chart modified from Jerry Richardson, *The Magic of Rapport* (Capitola, California: Meta Publications, 1987).

for key aspects of all that data your eyes and ears collect. Each of us gathers data differently. For some, the most important indicator of trouble is an expression on someone's face—a tightening of facial muscles, shifting of focal point, or other visual clues. For others, the key data is a shift in voice tone, pitch, or tempo that creates the subconscious-to-conscious message: "Something doesn't sound right here." For still others, the compiled data produces an uncertain sensation in the abdomen or a tightening in the chest that means "this doesn't feel right, I'd better check."

Whatever your processing system, the critical issue is, "How do I make sure unspoken messages are vivid enough, loud enough, or strong enough to get my attention?" For some, simply thinking about it may be enough to increase signal strength. For others, it will require sustained effort over time, reviewing past experiences, and reminding yourself how important it is to notice the "shift indicators" early. Like all new behaviors, this may seem awkward at first, but you will be surprised at how quickly you can integrate the skill of rapport-building into your repertoire once you decide to do so.

Cooperation, Not Submission

If you are good at counterexamples and the phrase "Yes, but . . ." comes as naturally as breathing, you may be thinking, "Yes, but I don't *have* to go through all this. I can reach my goals by just pressing forward. I don't have to do all this fancy stuff." And you are right. In the short term. The issue is effectiveness over time. If your style is to badger people into going along with you, you will find that, over time, fewer and fewer people will want to work with you.

You may be thinking, "What a relief! I only want to work with a chosen few!" Consider the implications of that stance. In a team-driven work environment, someone no one wants to work with has little job security. Similarly, to get opportunities to do the most interesting work you must be perceived as a team player who is willing to listen and relate to others.

Conclusion

Your goal in reading this book is to become a professional communicator; someone who believes that *the meaning of your communication is the response you get,* and who works to increase behavioral flexibility to produce more opportunities to attain desired results. Professional communicators understand the structure of effectiveness well enough to quickly diagnose when there are communication breakdowns and do something *different*. Paying attention to the other person's behavior gives you clues about what that something different might be.

As a professional communicator, you know that rapport is the basic currency of any relationship, the core of listening, and fundamental to responsiveness in the communication system. You also understand the learning process well enough to be patient and be fascinated by it. And you don't beat yourself up when you do not communicate as effectively as you might. Professional communicators keep learning! When you learn to manage your attention, you increase your ability to establish and maintain rapport with a wide variety of people. This increases your ability to establish mutual understanding in the New Workplace and get significant work done.

CHAPTER SEVEN

Recognizing and Reducing Resistance

Have you ever found out that someone was mad at you for reasons of which you were totally unaware? Have you come up with a brilliant technical solution that no one would implement? Or have you experienced hostility from someone who kept insisting he or she was just being "rational"? Ever see a project go down in flames because of infighting and politics? Or die a slow death because no one seemed to know what needed to be done next? Ever see two people stuck in a needlessly acrimonious debate that leads nowhere?

Purpose

Most of us say "yes" to at least several items on the list above. All those experiences are examples of failures to recognize and reduce resistance. Some of the resistance was active, some passive. Some belonged to you, and some belonged to other people. But all of it was resistance or, as Webster's defines it, "an opposing or retarding force,"[1] which prevented work from getting done. This chapter explores the dynamics, or syntax, of resistance and introduces tools that will help you manage it—in yourself and in others. It concludes the LINK section of our Model of Effectiveness.

Resistance: Response to Embarrassment or Threat

Some people thrive on resistance. Opposition gets their juices flowing and energizes them in positive ways. Most of us, however, find it embarrassing or threatening. Whatever our differences, all human beings have the same basic response to threat or embarrassment. As described in Chapter Four, we try to cover up the fact that we feel threatened or embarrassed. Then we cover up the fact that we are covering up by making the whole situa-

---

[1] *Webster's Seventh New Collegiate Dictionary* (Springfield, Mass.: G. & C. Merriam, 1969) 731.

tion undiscussable. Finally, we make the cover-up airtight by making the fact that it is undiscussable equally undiscussable. This self-sealing loop is called a "defensive routine."[2] No wonder things get bogged down! In truth, it is amazing we ever get any work done.

How can you manage resistance without triggering the defensive reflex? For openers, recognize that defensiveness is happening and quickly redefine or reframe it. Most of us have knee-jerk responses to resistance. Our own resistance makes us self-righteous or rigid; someone else's evokes our "fight or flight" response. Either way, the temptation is to resist the resistance, to increase the opposing force as a form of self-protection.

What happens when you resist resistance? Inevitably, the resistance escalates. And escalates. And escalates. It may be emotionally satisfying at the moment but, over time, it is usually destructive. How often have endings— to projects, relationships, friendships, marriages, partnerships—become bitter while both sides secretly thought, "I never meant for it to go this far?" Almost always, the parties got locked into a spiral of resisting resistance they did not know how to stop.

Redefining Resistance

Instead of experiencing (and thus defining) resistance as an indicator of potential threat or embarrassment, what if you looked at resistance as feedback? Or information? Or data? Or a symptom of lack of mutual understanding? Then, instead of thinking, "Boy, is that guy a jerk!" you could think, "Hmm, something isn't right here. What additional information do we need to exchange to get back on track?" What if you thought of resistance as evidence that what you are doing is not working, that you need to do something different to reach your goal? Obviously, "Hmm, I need to try a different approach here," is a more useful response than "Boy, would I like to shove that answer down his throat!"

In a sense, this is the mental equivalent of aikido, a martial art that views resistance as simply a force in motion. The art is to turn the force in the direction you want it to go. A sure way to fail is to try to block the force directly. Cowboys do not manage stampedes by getting in front of the herd and yelling "Stop!" Instead, they ride alongside the herd, then slowly move towards the front, closer and closer to the direction they want the herd to turn. By the time they reach the front, the herd is already moving in a new direction.

---

[2] Chris Argyris, *Knowledge for Action, A Guide to Overcoming Barriers to Organizational Change*, (San Francisco, California: Jossey-Bass, 1993) 134–149.

One powerful result of reframing resistance into a need for additional information is that it brings control over your behavior back to you. If you are in the grip of your "fight or flight" response, you are totally in a reactive mode. There is little room for the proactive moves that mark someone who knows his or her goals and has the flexibility to try many paths to reach them. By switching instead to *curiosity,* a mindset that says "I wonder what's going on here?" you give yourself the opportunity to regain a proactive stance. No one else is pushing your buttons. Right away the power of resistance to derail you diminishes. The downward spiral of resistance halts.

Recognizing Resistance

"Well, all right," you might be thinking. "I can see that. But if I'm calm, cool, and collected, and the other person isn't, won't I be mismatching— and irritating—them?" Good point! The first step in managing resistance is to recognize it early. That starts with recognizing your own patterns so that you can become sensitive to how other people are similar and different. You can be conscious of the other person's early signals, and match the change in their energy. Mentally, you are cool and calm. Behaviorally, you respond to the changes you detect either by matching intensity or rate of speech, or by asking the other person what has just changed.

The early warning signs of resistance are microscopic moves—increased muscle tension in the face and scalp, for example, resulting in bulges at the back of the jaw, a visible rigidity in the muscles around the mouth or in the neck, tightening of the muscles around the eyes, changes in pupil size. Or there might be shifts in breathing rate or, even more subtle, interruption of digestive processes that result in arms folded across the chest.

Because we share the desire to cover up such responses, we try not to show those micromoves. Of course, all we really do is shrink them. It is impossible *not* to communicate. What happens however, is that our communication perplexes anyone who is not an expert at reading our signals. (Ever notice how your spouse or significant other *always* knows when you are irritated, even when you are sure you are hiding it?) Since the physical manifestations are *so* microscopic, all others get is the feeling something is wrong. Thus, the escalation of resistance is under way despite your efforts!

What to Do and What Not to Do

Remember the last time *you* seriously resisted someone else? Imagine that there is a tiny coach sitting on that person's shoulder. What is the worst thing the coach could tell that person to do, the one action guaranteed to raise your resistance rate exponentially? On the other hand, what is the best advice the coach could give, the move that would cool you down enough to engage in real conversation? Rank the list in Figure 7-1 of bests and worsts we have collected from years of working with Syntax participants and add any we have left out.

Worst:	Best:
☐ Patronize me	☐ Listen carefully
☐ Tell me again what you just said	☐ Show you really care
☐ Ignore me	☐ Leave me alone until I calm down
☐ Try to placate me	☐ Ask me questions that probe my reasoning
☐ Tell me you don't care what I think	☐ Verify what you heard me say
☐ Insult me	☐ Go back and re-check the goals of the conversation
☐ Walk away from me	☐
☐ Tell me I'm wrong	
☐ "My way or the highway"	
☐ Say the same things louder	
☐	

FIGURE 7-1: WORST AND BEST RESPONSES TO RESISTANCE

Notice that similar actions, i.e. "Walk away from me," and "Leave me alone until I calm down," are on both lists. What some people experience as room to breathe and think may cause others to feel abandoned. Timing, a sense of the other person's preferences, and the manner in which you leave the person alone, all determine what will work when.

The best way to handle people who resist you is to *meet them where they are.* The worst way is to stay focused on your own point of view and *lead too soon,* since this is usually experienced as profound disrespect.

Know Your Own Hot Buttons

Before you can stay mentally cool and collected, you need to be able to manage your own resistant responses. Set up a signal system that allows you to neutralize your own resistance. The trick is to notice when the experience of feeling disrespected begins. What happens physiologically at that point? Some people's jaws literally "get tight." Some feel a pulse in their temples. Others experience a churning in their stomach, or an increase in blood pressure. Often these things occur at an unconscious level, so we are unaware that we are feeling angry and resistant. By the time we are aware, we may be in too deep to easily let go. Thus, the ability to detect those physical indicators early—first in ourselves and then in others—can be extraordinarily useful in managing resistance.

The more quickly you respond to your nonverbal seismograph, the better you will prevent escalation. When in doubt, ask questions, even if you don't know what to ask. For example, "I have the feeling something is not quite right here. Are there issues I'm not aware of?" or similar inquiries, honestly asked, can help surface resistance before it gets inflated. Obviously, do not ask a probing question if you are not prepared to deal with the answer. However, when you don't ask difficult questions, you let fear of the responses deprive you of useful and timely opportunities to resolve real problems.

Handling Resistance

Once you have identified resistance and reframed it for yourself, there are specific behaviors for reducing resistance (see Figure 7-2). They are in order from matching to leading. First, meet the person where he or she is, openly acknowledging the resistance, issue, or problem. Always, always, *match before you lead!* You **cannot** reduce resistance until you recognize it. Start with *verifying* the current situation.

For example, "If I understand the situation correctly, you feel that the specs were faulty to begin with, that you tried several times to have them clarified and got nowhere, and that you then went ahead and did it exactly as it was written. Is that a fair description of the situation?" If the answer is negative, restate your understanding or, better yet, ask which parts were inaccurate and get the other person to respond.

```
┌─────────────────────────────────────────────────────────┐
│                                                           │
│  MATCH                                                    │
│                                                           │
│    VERIFY              WHAT I UNDERSTAND YOU               │
│                        TO MEAN IS . . . IS THAT           │
│                        RIGHT?                             │
│                                                           │
│    ALIGN               LET ME LOOK AT IT FROM             │
│                        YOUR POINT OF VIEW.                │
│                                                           │
│  SLIGHT LEAD                                              │
│                                                           │
│    PROBE               TELL ME MORE ABOUT                 │
│                        WHAT CONCERNS YOU.                 │
│                                                           │
│  LEAD                                                     │
│                                                           │
│    PHRASE              HOW CAN WE WORK IT                  │
│                        OUT SO THAT (your needs            │
│                        and my needs can both be           │
│                        met)?                              │
│                                                           │
│    ASK                 WHAT WILL IT TAKE TO               │
│                        (include both concerns)?           │
│                                                           │
└─────────────────────────────────────────────────────────┘
```

FIGURE 7-2: RESISTANCE REDUCERS

If the answer is affirmative, you have a couple of choices for your next move. If emotions are running high, *aligning* with the other person is useful. That means seeing things from the other person's point of view. Responses such as, "So, from your point of view . . .," or "It sounds like you're concerned about . . ." convey your willingness to understand.

You can sometimes make a nice physical corollary move when you are *aligning.* Where possible, move to a parallel position so that when you "look at it from their point of view," you are standing next to them and looking in the same direction. Even when using the auditory or kinesthetic version, "Let me tune in to how this might sound to you," or "Let me get a feel for this from your position," moving to a parallel physical position conveys a powerful message about your willingness to share the experience. It says you are willing to make extra effort to understand their situation. It is hard to stay in active resistance when someone is clearly willing to come more than half way!

Once you have matched, a slight lead may be effective. Probing is a possible alternative to, or next step after, aligning. It is essentially an information-gathering move. If you are not sure what the issues are, a gentle "Tell me more about what concerns you" can do wonders. If you are clear about some of the situation, but not all of it, use the "specifics" and "limits" questions outlined in Chapters Eight and Nine.

The point is to understand that resistance indicates a different map of the situation from yours, and it is your job to locate those differences. It can be humbling, because sometimes you discover that your comprehension of the situation was not as thorough as you had assumed!

Thoughts and Feelings *Are* Data

In the context of communication, thoughts and feelings are data, every bit as much as so-called "hard facts." When you do not attend to thoughts and feelings, you lose wholehearted commitment and settle for something between resignation and passive resistance. This is one of the most powerful aspects of *"meet people where they are before you lead."* In doing so, you enable obstacles, whether thoughts or feelings, to be removed.

In technical environments, we often fear that thoughts and feelings, if expressed, will replace rational analysis and problem-solving. In fact, the opposite is true. If forced underground, thoughts and feelings begin to take on a sneaky life of their own and may leak out in sarcastic comments and backbiting. This can poison the atmosphere as subtly and gradually as air pollution. Communication becomes polluted, there is not enough of it, and channels become clogged with the debris of hostility and frustration. Defensive routines predominate, truth-telling vanishes, the Blame Frame prevails, and less and less is accomplished. This takes a toll at every level. Organizations once believed to be invincible and permanent collapse under their own weight. People in them experience high levels of frustration, bitterness, and despair.

Two important points: First, addressing thoughts and feelings as data is not the same as capitulating to someone else's desires. Decisions still require a sound technical basis in the New Workplace. However, decisions that address only technical issues may be undermined or overlooked. Quality solutions are created only when you address both aspects of the situation. That is when you have real mutual understanding.

Second, thoughts and feelings have a logic every bit as implacable as a good problem-solving process. They are not really irrational, confused, or illogical. We experience them that way primarily because we do not fully understand their roots. When people can articulate their thoughts and feelings without fear of repercussion, it can be as orderly and logical as any other aspect of the engineering process—*if* you remember that people have their own experiences and their own points of view.

That is the reason *probing* is necessary. You cannot establish mutual understanding without exploring the other person's experiences. Remember the concept of "go slow to go fast." Hearing out someone else's issues thoroughly prevents unwarranted assumptions that derail all your efforts to lower resistance and get things back on track. These ideas are in concert with one of Stephen Covey's "habits of highly effective people": "Seek first to understand and then to be understood."[3] Often we are so focused on making everyone understand *our* point of view, we do not bother to find out if we really understand theirs.

Uncharted Territory: Uncovering Mental Models and Beliefs

All of us make assumptions about how the world works, what is rightfully ours, and how people are going to behave. We are mostly unaware of those assumptions; they are just embedded in the background of all our thinking and behavior. Often, however, they form the roots of resistance, and becoming aware of them can make us uncomfortable. It can also provide significant impetus for learning and change. It is difficult to achieve shared understanding with others unless we understand how our own assumptions operate.

The process of managing resistance is one of uncovering mental models. It can operate at the level of discovering missing details. Or it can exist at the level of discovering parts of the model that involve your beliefs about life. Either way, genuine respectfulness is required; nothing less permits an open exchange of information.

Taking the Lead

Only when you are sure you can see, hear, and feel the situation from the other person's point of view—including thoughts, feelings and mental mod-

---

[3] Stephen R. Covey, *Seven Habits of Highly Effective People* (New York: Simon & Schuster, 1989) 235–260.

els—and confirm that *with* her or him, can you begin to resolve the problem. These next steps involve taking the lead. One move might be *phrasing,* asking some variation of "How can we work it out so that your needs get met and mine get met as well?"

Notice the structure of that inquiry: Unless you make it clear that meeting the other person's needs is your *foremost* goal, you run the risk of escalating the resistance. Asking "How can we work it out so that *my* needs get met and so do yours?" may sound the same as "How can we work it out so that my needs get met?" Not much of an offer, especially if your goal is to contain or lower resistance. This is one instance where "the meaning of your communication" will certainly be "the response you get!"

Sometimes probing reveals major hurdles to any useful resolution. In that case, a *phrasing* response could negate all your rapport-building since the answer might be, "There's no way!" Instead, try *asking*: "I grant that there are serious obstacles to doing this job the way we would both like to see it done. For the moment, let's set aside the issue of properly written specifications. What else would it take to get the job done well?" This is an invitation to brainstorm some of the situational constraints, to discover alternatives. When everyone is fully aware of the difficulties, it is tough to formulate creative options. By setting aside the limiting effect of those constraining forces, you can explore a wider range of possible resolutions.

Effectively reducing resistance is a clear-cut opportunity to practice a variety of verbal and nonverbal actions. Congruence is very important. If your voice tone, inflection, and body language do not reflect genuine commitment to working things out, step out of the situation until you *can* work from a problem-solving frame. If your own thoughts and feelings prohibit that, you need to express them to yourself or others before you can switch frames.

Argyris' case study process is helpful in these situations: Clients write a description of a frustrating dialogue they have had or expect to have in a column on the right-hand side of the page. On the left side they write out their thoughts and feelings during such a conversation. Sharing this is a way to surface many of the unspoken issues, mental models, and beliefs that prevent problems from really being solved.[4]

People with a high commitment to working things out may be willing to join you in this kind of openness. In any case, using the process for yourself may expose ways that your own thinking continues to feed resistance.

---

[4] Chris Argyris, *op. cit.*

Conclusion

Resistance is a reality of life, especially while we are in the difficult transition to the New Workplace. Our effectiveness in any situation often hinges on how we respond to and manage resistance. Being curious rather than irritated, flexible rather than focused, patient rather than condescending, gives us room to maneuver. Careful use of resistance reducers gets things back on track and moves us toward mutually beneficial solutions.

CHAPTER EIGHT

Just the Facts, Please—
Not Your Interpretation!

How much of your job involves getting and giving information, from getting and discussing specifications to getting and giving assignments, progress reports, audits, test runs, and completions? Every step of a technical process requires the transmission and reception of information. The better the quality of that information—the more accurate, undistorted, detailed, and relevant—the more smoothly the work process flows. Personal information management, then, is at the heart of the modern technical or other professional's work. You must gather, organize and interpret the reams of information that surround you at almost every working moment.

Purpose

We will now begin examining the INFORM part of the Syntax Model. The purpose of this chapter is to give you specific guidelines about how to elicit facts, benefit from the knowledge of others, and convey your knowledge to others.

Given the team-based nature of work today, the source of much information is inevitably other people. The information management process breaks down when we do not receive high-quality information. Information distorted by assumptions, biases, and interpretations produces erroneous judgments and conclusions. This process is almost inevitable. Highly effective people are good at compensating for it.

Some of your questioning habits are excellent for getting (and giving) clean information. Others may not serve as well. In this chapter, you get insight into the communication process, recognition of the crucial difference between perception and interpretation, and useful, hands-on, nuts-and-bolts tools for gathering high-quality information from others.

What We Are Trying to Communicate Is . . .

Consider how the communication process works. We have far more experience than we ever articulate. Our bodies constantly register information about the sights, sounds, smells, feelings, and tastes of those experiences, yet we are rarely conscious of that process. For the most part, data is simply stored in the format in which it is received—as smells, physical and emotional sensations, sounds, and pictures.

Coached properly, we can retrieve a substantial portion of that information. In the 1992 movie *Sneakers*, Robert Redford leads a band of aging hackers who make their living testing bank security systems. At one point he is captured by the bad guys, who tie him up, throw him in the trunk of a car, and take him out to the country to meet their boss. After the meeting he is returned to the city the same way.

Back at headquarters, he wishes aloud that there was some way to figure out where they had taken him. "Perhaps we can," says a member of the band who is blind. "What did you hear?"

"Hear? I couldn't hear anything! I was blindfolded and stuffed in the trunk of a car!" exclaims Redford.

"I know that. What did you hear? What did the road sound like?" replies the blind man. Slowly and patiently he enables Redford to turn off his dominant visual and kinesthetic channels and re-access his less-conscious auditory channel. Based on the data stored there, they recreate the trip and locate the bad guys' headquarters. It is a great example of how much information we gather unconsciously.

Which is just as well. If you *had* to articulate all that data, it might take three hours to describe how you slept last night. What is important is to understand how much data you *can* draw on if you have to, and to be aware of the transformation of data in the communication process.

Did you ever wake up and try to describe a particularly rich and vivid dream? Often, you are acutely aware that you are not capturing it, not conveying the intricacy, color, and power of the dream. But in the rush to capture some of it before the memory fades, you grasp whatever words are handy.

This happens most of the time we are communicating. There are dozens of ways to describe anything. To a large extent, our choices are constrained by what we have paid conscious attention to. We filter and alter a lot of information at an unconscious level; we need to in order to survive. If we had to pay attention to *all* the data, we would be hard pressed to accomplish anything. Many psychiatrists believe psychotic episodes occur when people lose the ability to sort and filter information, and are forced to respond to all of it.

Probing Surface Statements

As we sort through our rich and chaotic experience base, our preconceptions, beliefs, needs and concerns limit what we actually pay attention to. Next, we must select labels—words—for the information we choose. English offers an exceptional selection of words, although it is richer in some areas than others. It does not, for example, have as many words for snow as the Inuit language of Alaska, nor as many words for love as French.

We make unconscious choices as to which parts of experience we put into words and then, out of the pool of all words that might apply, we choose (usually unconsciously) the ones we think best describe the experience. Unless, of course, we choose the same words we always use or whichever ones are handy at the moment. The final selection of words results in a "surface statement," a thin representation of the richness embedded in an experience (Figure 8-1).

All of this normally goes on at lightning speed inside our brain, well outside of conscious awareness, although we may consciously cast about for a word or phrase to express something we feel strongly about. It is occurring every moment we are speaking. We bridge the chasm between experience and the words used to describe it constantly and with remarkable success. And we periodically fall into the chasm with a resounding thud. The skill of the effective communicator is to recognize when it is important to probe beneath the surface of a statement to check the experience.

As a rule of thumb, take the time to check what the other person meant when the cost of *not* checking is more than you are willing to pay. Once the skill of checking assumptions becomes second nature, you will do it effortlessly, easily and often, wasting less energy to learn more useful information. What skilled communicators do is to separate raw data—the stored information collected by the senses—from how it is interpreted.

Forms of Filtering

Increasing the difficulty of capturing the richness of experience in words is the fact that mental models dictate what we experience. Recent biological

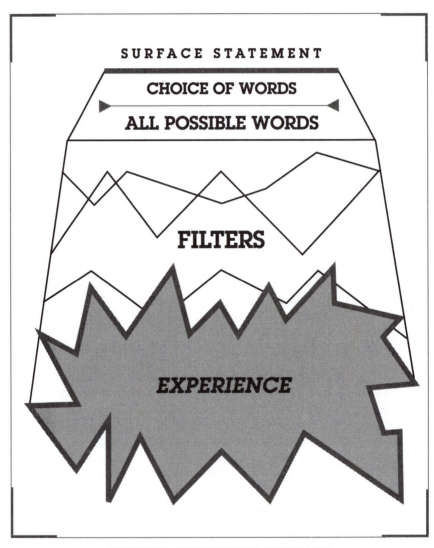

FIGURE 8-1: LANGUAGE AND EXPERIENCE

research indicates that 20 percent of our comprehension of external stimuli comes directly from those stimuli; 80 percent comes from preexisting memories, beliefs, and filters.[1]

Three filters explain how two people who are in the same place at the same time, ostensibly having the same experience, can have dramatically

---

[1] Humberto Maturana and Francisco Varela, *The Tree of Knowledge* (Boston: Shambala, 1992).

different experiences. The first filter is *deletion.* While common wisdom has it that "seeing is believing," in reality "believing is seeing."

With rare exceptions, we experience what our belief structure (that 80 percent) permits. If we do not believe it is possible to improve the way things are done, no amount of "proof" will change our mind. Similarly, someone who is afraid of conflict will "not hear" provocative remarks or the anger in someone else's voice. Everyone—including you—has blind spots. They cannot be eradicated, but they can shrink over time.

The second information-processing filter is *distortion.* Slightly more subtle than deletion, it involves taking information in and then shifting the emphasis or altering the data so that it better fits our preconceptions. This often happens with information that challenges our fundamental notions of how the world works, our so-called "paradigms."

For example, people involved in the Total Quality movement tend to notice when others are stuck in their old paradigms. The "we've-always-done-it-this-way-and-it-has-worked-for-us" mentality resists the introduction of quality tools and techniques. Remember, however, that few are really good at "paradigm-busting." It is always easier to see the changes that others need to make than to realize that we are stuck ourselves. Managing the tendency to distort information so as to reinforce our beliefs requires constant effort.

The third significant filter is *generalization.* Here you take one experience, frequently your first with an individual or a situation, and make it applicable to all similar experiences. This is an important skill for learning; indeed, one of the most important. If we were unable to generalize and had to, for example, rediscover the function of a door knob every time we encountered one, life would be tedious indeed. Yet, generalization is a double-edged sword: It can serve us or sever us from important information—especially when our generalizations form our expectations! The risk is that we will overlook future possibilities because we are blinded by the past. How often are new technologies delayed or killed because people cannot see the possibilities they represent?

Sensory Description

Describing something, someone, or an event is an act of making distinctions. You note and comment on how something is different from—more, less, louder, rougher, softer, brighter, duller, larger, smaller than—something else. It has been observed that all perception, all human information processing, is really a process of making distinctions.[2] Cultures generate

---

[2] Gregory Bateson, *Mind and Nature* (New York: E.P. Dutton, 1979).

language and behavior to describe the distinctions that matter and emphasize what is important. The Inuit of Alaska have many words for snow, and the Kikuyu of Kenya can recognize their own cattle from hundreds of others.

Thus, when you describe behavior, what you are really describing are *changes* in behavior. Most of the time, we make semiconscious snap decisions due to changes we observe in others' behavior. Much of our wisdom and many shortcuts are embedded in those instantaneous interpretations. As it turns out, much wisdom can also be lost when we interpret so quickly.

Awareness enables you to detect subtle changes in others' responses that indicate whether you are moving toward your desired outcome with them, or farther away. If you understand this continuous process, your own behavior can be more flexible and responsive. To slow down the act of interpretation and increase awareness of what we are interpreting from, we use *sensory-based language*. Sensory-based language reports the data your senses gather without comment or interpretation. It presents as close a representation of what was seen and heard as can be put into words.

Here is a sensory description: "John pointed towards the door and said, rapidly and loudly, 'Anyone who doesn't wish to make a 100 percent commitment to this project is welcome to leave now.' He leaned back in his chair, took a breath, and picked up his clipboard."

The same scene, in interpretive description: "John laid down the law. He started right away to provide leadership. When the project team accepted his challenge, the real work began." It does not describe exactly what happened, but it does convey the meaning the speaker ascribed to the scene.

Uses of Sensory Description

The best way to convey what you want someone to do is to demonstrate it; if you cannot, then you need to describe what you have done or want done in sensory-based language. It is as close as words can come to depicting what we experienced or what we intend. Similarly, the better your sensory description of a desired outcome, the easier it is to orient yourself and others toward that outcome.

Sensory description can also help you focus your attention on the other person, rather than on your own goal or agenda. The next time you listen to someone uninteresting or irritating, experiment with sensory description. Describe to yourself *exactly* what you are hearing—words, tone, tempo, as well as gestures, and micro-movements. For example: *He is raising his left hand to his right ear and pulling downward on it. The muscles around his eyes are tightening, deepening the creases outside of his eyes. Vertical wrinkles appear in his forehead between his eyebrows. There are bulges at the back of the jaw. His lips have gotten thinner, and wrinkles are appearing around his mouth.* Without determining whether your subject has indigestion or is getting very angry, you will naturally pay more attention to the sensory data and automatically use the information when you need it. In addition, you will reduce the tendency to add your filters.

Managing Your Attention

When you are lost in interpretation or making judgments or wondering why you lack rapport or are frustrated in the attempt to reach your goal, it is a good time to use sensory description inside your mind. Notice facial movements and gestures, what you hear, and what others are saying. This pulls you out of your own thoughts and puts you in sync again. It will, in turn, facilitate movement toward the goal.

Deletion, distortion, and generalization are unavoidable. Indeed, you need them to move effectively through the day. At times, they create situations which massively blindside you. By developing acute awareness, you can learn to compensate for them. Learning to pay attention to sensory data keeps you grounded and better able to test for deleted, distorted, or generalized information. As long as you remember that *no two human beings experience the same thing in the same way*, you will remember to explore what others are actually experiencing, rather than your own version of it.

Getting Down to Details

People say exactly what they mean—but they do not say all that they mean. By recognizing words and word patterns that indicate there is more to know, you can ask quick and efficient questions. You may ask, "How do I know what information I need?" It depends on your goal. By keeping your outcome in mind and stating it clearly, you minimize irrelevant conversation and consistently bring the conversation back to the goal.

Uncovering Information

Filters damage data in two major ways: We delete, create, or hallucinate details based on our own experience, and we imagine limitations that do not exist. Both kinds of damage have major implications on the smooth flow of work. For example, engineering and accounting standards for various procedures develop variances over time within organizations. When people move to new organizations, they carry those variances with them often believing those are the "right way" to do things.

Likewise, assumptions about what is possible, generalized from past experiences, preclude solutions that can save thousands of hours and dollars if checked for accuracy *in the current situation*. For example, company policy precludes use of outside engineering consultants. However, exceptions have been allowed when it was proven that the needed expertise did not exist in-house, and that the time required to develop it would destroy the project. But no one knows about the exceptions, and an important project fails because it lacked a critical resource.

In all cases, looking beneath surface statements to discover the original experience is the way to make sure everyone is working with clean information. In the first place, you recover information that has been deleted, distorted, or generalized by filters. In the second, which we address in detail in Chapter Nine, you discover whether or not assumed limits are real. In both cases, make sure you have built the relationship (linked) first. Unless you have established rapport, these tools can be irritating and exasperating to the other person. With rapport, they are simply part of your work together and enhance your value.   .

What and How Questions

We often refer to somebody's mindset, their experience of the world, as a "map." Everyone has a different map, a full set of visual, auditory, and kinesthetic (feeling) representations of experience. Each person's map is rich and unique, reflecting his or her own sense of the world, experiences, and beliefs. When we put these experiences into words, we selectively delete, distort, and generalize, if only to reduce the number of words it takes to convey a message.

In a conversation, you hear only the surface level of what a person means. By being aware of someone's patterns in presenting information and asking "what" and "how" questions to understand what is behind them, you can examine the parts you need to know about. If you want to understand the meaning behind someone's words, listen to exactly what the person says and then ask about specific parts.

If your goal is clear, you will know what information you need. If you have linked effectively, it will open clear channels of communication. Listening to someone speak, you can sense what is missing and when to ask questions. Ask more "what" and "how" questions than you normally ask; the results will surprise you.

Nominalizations

Another tool for quickly gathering relevant, intelligent information is to recognize *nominalizations*. Nominalizations are verbs made into nouns, umbrella words that represent complex activity or something in motion. Examples from *Smart Work* include "plan," "link," "understanding," and "resistance." They are deceptive in that it sounds as though you are talking about an object, when you are actually talking about a dynamic process.

To de-nominalize what you have heard, first notice the nominalization. Any "thing" that you cannot picture, hear, or feel concretely is a likely candidate. Then turn the nominalization back into a verb by asking questions to fill in. "Who is doing what to whom and in what way?" In the example, "We don't have any understanding on this point," "understanding" sounds like an object. In fact, it is a verb needing to have its subject *and* object restored. Inquiring "Who understanding what?" gets you valuable detail about what the speaker is expressing.

There are several benefits to uncovering nominalizations. Obviously, you get more information when you attach subjects and objects to abstract symbols. In addition, de-nominalizing reduces hidden assumptions. When you hear and accept nominalizations as things, you are likely to fill in the blanks, and make assumptions about the statement's meaning.

Some nominalizations are more emotionally laden than others; all nominalizations invite a great deal of subjectivity. Think about "efficiency" or "productivity" or "respect." Consider the term "management." In our haste to converse, we throw these words around carelessly. It may not matter if we have different interpretations, because the goal of the exchange is fairly loose. When you say, "I'm feeling a lot of frustration about management's indecision," you may only want your feelings acknowledged. The listener does not need to know exactly what is frustrating you and who in management is not deciding what. On the other hand, if they want to influence you and improve your attitude, good questions would rapidly reveal the pain beneath the words.

By envisioning words as locations on someone's map, realizing that those words are abstractions of fuller experiences, asking questions and de-nominalizing words, you ascertain the meaning below the words. You get closer to the experience, create a shared map and establish a solid basis for mutual understanding.

Consumer Protection Warning: Project startups and other new beginnings are especially good times to check nominalizations. However, do not take de-nominalizing to extremes. Pay attention to context. If the shared meaning is already clear, questioning the "obvious" may make you seem a pest.

Specifics Questions

The first step to recovering lost data is to recognize words almost certain to carry embedded meaning. To a degree, this is true of all words. For example, "The dog runs." One person's "dog" is an old, small, fat, splotchy brown-and-white mutt; yours is a high-stepping, long-haired pointer. Yours "runs" in long, graceful loping strides; theirs "runs" in a gawky, uneven wobble with great wheezing gasps.

If even such a simple sentence forms completely different mental images, imagine what happens with words like "truth," "justice," "empowerment," "respect," "trust," "rightsizing," "re-engineering" and "ethics." Our meanings for those words are produced by a rich experiential data base of background, interactions, beliefs, values, and concerns.

Other words that need further exploration are the converse of nominalizations: nouns that have been turned into verbs. Much current business jargon fits that category: The noun "impact" has become the verb "to impact," the phrase "the right size" has become "to rightsize," the noun "rationale" has become the verb "to rationalize." These words also bear a wealth of meaning. You can get valuable information when you tactfully probe both nouns-into-verbs and verbs-into-nouns.

NOT "Why . . . ?"

To uncover deleted, distorted, and generalized information, start with "specifics questions," the old newspaper litany of "who, what, where, when, how?" "What did you see, hear or feel that led you to that conclusion?" That way you can discover the sensory data that was stored and interpreted. Adding "specifically" or "exactly" makes it clear that you are seeking precisely the details that led to the conclusion.

Notice, please, we omit "why" from the list of questions. In Western culture, "why" has a combative or pejorative connotation. Even though children repeatedly ask "why," adults usually associate it with criticism from parents: "*Why* did you do that?"

Try this experiment: Ask a friend to tell you about something he or she has done recently. Ask "Why did you do that?" or "Why did you go there?" or five or six similar "why" questions. Notice what it does both to your rapport and the kind of information (detailed and specific, or high-level, historical, or emotional) this generates. Then ask to hear the same story again, this time asking only "what," "how," and "who" questions. Again, notice the kind of information you get.

"Why" elicits history, reasons, justifications, rationalizations, and sometimes wisdom. It gets you interpretations. If that is what you want, then "why" is the right question to ask. If you want to discover what was seen, heard, or felt that led to those conclusions in order to form *your own conclusions,* it is more useful to ask "what" and "how" questions. Then, *you* can interpret and not accept someone else's interpretation.

Those with training in quality tools and theory may be thinking, "OK, what about 'The Five Whys?' What about 'root cause analysis?'" Root cause analysis is exactly what we are supporting: what data were people working from when the problem developed? However, a process of uncovering that data which results in needless antagonism contributes to further delay. "The Five Whys" were developed in a different cultural context, one in which enormous attention is paid to relationship. The context and connotations of "why" are not the same in Western cultures as in the East. The message here is NOT to *never* use "why". It *is* to think about the kind of information you get when you use "why" and change if you are not getting what you need.

Let's look at a case study:

Mary's statement: "This situation is hopeless."

You: "Why?"

Mary: "Because they never deliver under tight deadlines, and Jim always goes to pieces under pressure."

Note the immediate shift into the Blame Frame (see Chapter Four) and reinforcement of despair. Contrast the results of "why" with "what and how":

Mary's statement: "This situation is hopeless."

Your Syntax Response: "What specifically about the situation is hopeless?"

Mary: "Well, they don't have the engineering strength, nor, I believe, the determination to deliver."

You: "How *exactly* is their engineering strength lacking?"

Mary: "They're short two people, and the guys they do have are computer science experts rather than EEs. This effort is as much a hardware issue as software."

You: "Ah, so there are serious staffing issues on this team. That's very useful to know. We'll need to inform the project manager. He may be able to send us some additional bodies. *Exactly* what have you seen or heard that leads you to conclude they lack the determination to deliver?"

Mary: "Well, I've worked with three people on that team before, and they are the kind of people who get so fascinated by possibilities that they find it hard to quit exploring and start delivering."

You: "What do they do when they get fascinated by possibilities?"

Mary: "Research, endless research. Jim benchmarked for six months on the Forsythe project. Granted, he brought back a lot of very useful information, but it drove me nuts. Every time I wanted to get started, he'd add in new information that I'd have to deal with."

You: "So part of the issue is the fact that you like to get rolling fast and run by the seat of your pants, and these guys want to do a lot of fact-gathering first?"

Mary: "Yeah, well, I guess you could put it like that."

Now you are in a position to draw your own conclusions. If the situation requires immediate action, you may accept Mary's judgment as valid and helpful. If, on the other hand, the situation represents an opportunity to do cutting-edge work and benchmarking "state-of-the-art" would contribute significantly, you now have data from which to draw a different conclusion.

Note the assumption that you knew what situation Mary was talking about. Under other circumstances, you might have had to inquire, "What situation is hopeless?" before exploring further. As you improve, you can begin to practice "economy of motion" drills—combining all possible questions into one all-encompassing inquiry. For example, upon hearing Mary's original statement, you might ask; "What situation is hopeless and how is it hopeless?" Or even the ungrammatical yet efficient, "What situation is hopeless how?"

Let's look at another example:

Joe's statement: "They won't do the job right."

You: "Why won't they do the job right?"

Joe: "They have an attitude about our stuff and always set out to sabotage us."

Notice how the "why" question accepts the assumption that "they" won't do the job right. It allows Joe's biases to serve as operational wisdom. Contrast it with this:

Joe's statement: "They won't do the job right."

You: "Who *specifically* won't do what job, and what *exactly* constitutes 'right'?"

Joe: "Boy, you ask weird questions! The automation department won't design an effective cell manufacturing set-up for the new processes we're getting into."

You: "I can see where that would be a serious problem, given how much we've invested to get those processes on-line fast. What *exactly* have you seen and heard that leads you to believe that?"

Joe: "Well, I was talking to a buddy of mine over in tool and die. He said the automation group is a bunch of wise-ass know-it-alls who talk big and don't deliver."

You: "Hmmm. How *specifically* does your buddy know that?"

Joe: "Er, uh, well, I don't exactly know. Maybe he had some prior experience with them?"

You: "Perhaps we ought to find out a little more before we accept his opinion as the final word?"

Joe: "Well, yeah, I guess so."

Again the goal is for *you* to determine the specific behavioral data—what has been seen, heard, and felt—that led to conclusions so you can make your own decisions. Especially under time pressure, you must make a conscious effort to overcome the tendency to accept the interpretations of others as fact.

Conclusion

There is an old folk saying that "the devil is in the details." Perhaps not in the details themselves, but in the inability to move large numbers of details accurately from one mind to another. In the New Workplace, with its time pressures and lack of hierarchy, the need to move those details is increasing exponentially. No doubt you appreciate the complexity of the process. The tools described in this chapter—recognizing filters, distinguishing sensory description from interpretation, asking what and how—may seem simple; however, they are only simple to talk about. Using them, applying them consistently and naturally, is complex indeed.

CHAPTER NINE

Moving Past
Self-Imposed Limits

Sometimes you feel sheer frustration while trying to communicate with someone. You appear to be exchanging facts, and yet something is blocking progress. There seems to be a ripple in the fabric of reality. Yet neither of you is consciously throwing obstacles in the way of the communication.

The problem may come from the way certain phrases can distort the facts, a phenomenon called "sleight of mind." There are certain ways of thinking that unnecessarily limit the possibilities for action or problem-solving. These mental patterns are so common that, without the symptom of frustration, we may not notice them at all.

Purpose

In addition to gathering details to capture filtered information, you can explore the assumed limitations of the situation, also revealed by language choices. This chapter continues to develop the INFORM section of the Syntax Model. Here you will find verbal moves to explore these limitations and determine which are real and which are imaginary. There is also a section on learning to verify—to systematically confirm mutual understanding at every opportunity and build consensus for cooperation.

Letting Go of Limits

By relinquishing limiting verbal patterns, you more accurately present the facts. Notice how much information a listener receives from, "We've sent up four different proposals about the type of new hardware that we need. Management has refused each request, with different explanations each time. Thus, I believe that it is highly unlikely that a fifth proposal could get funded."

Compare that to, "There's no point. Management never gives us what we need." As a technical consultant, which would give you a platform from which to work? Although the facts in the situation have not changed, the first example deals with specifics, and the second deals with generalizations. With the first, it might be possible to find out under what conditions management *would* approve the purchase of new hardware.

We have already examined the concept of "mental maps." A person's mental map determines what possibilities he or she perceives in a given situation. While not consciously eliminating options, people who have experienced a situation as *always* being a certain way, or think that their ideas would *never* be accepted, automatically fail to consider other possibilities. Such thinking patterns grow out of experience. Useful at one time, they have now become traps. People with these patterns may also discourage others from trying something creative. After all, why try if you know it can't work?

Common Kinds of Limits

Figure 9-1 presents six common kinds of limits: *universals, necessities, impossibles, mindreading, cause-effect,* and *either/or.* Each limit has its own typical language pattern.

Universals contain the words "all" or "every," as in "Everyone does it that way." The assumption behind universals is that universality justifies accepting the limitation.

Necessities hide behind words like "have to" or "must," as in "It must be done this way." The limit is in the assumed lack of choice. "It must be done by noon" is a typical statement of necessity.

Impossibles indicate that there is absolutely no way something can be done. They are revealed by words such as "can't" or "impossible." "That can't be done" is a typical impossibles statement.

The next three patterns are harder to spot, particularly when they correspond to your own habits of thinking. They are important because they distort the relationship between one thing, or one person, and another.

Mindreading is an implicit command masked by unsubstantiated third-party attributions. Phrases like "he thinks" or "they feel" imply that you *must* respond to what you imagine "he" or "they" think or feel, rather than what "he" or "they" actually said or did.

Cause-effect occurs when people give over power to other people or forces beyond their control. They believe that they are helpless to resist or alter their responses. The language pattern is "He/she/they/it make(s) me . . ." as in "He makes me crazy," or "She makes me mad when she is late," or "It makes me sick when they do that."

UNIVERSALS

WHEN THEY SAY: YOU ASK
"All . . ." "Every . . ."   "All?" "Every(one) (time)?"

IMPOSSIBLES

WHEN THEY SAY: YOU ASK:
"Can't . . ."   "What prevents (you) (us)
"Impossible . . ."   from . . .?"

NECESSITIES

WHEN THEY SAY: YOU ASK:
"Have to . . ." "Must . . ."   "What would happen if
                                  (we) (you) (they) didn't . . .?"

MINDREADING

WHEN THEY SAY: YOU ASK:
"They think (feel) . . ."   "How do you know they
                                  think (feel) that way?"

CAUSE-EFFECT

WHEN THEY SAY: YOU ASK
"They make me (us) . . ."   "How, specifically, do they
                                  make you (us) do that?"

EITHER/OR

WHEN THEY SAY: YOU ASK
"It's either ____ or ____"   "What other options might
                                  there be?"

FIGURE 9-1: INFORMATION-GATHERING QUESTIONS TO PROBE LIMITS

Either/or assumes a binary world. Things are right or wrong, black or white, there are only two alternatives in any situation. "Either we meet specs or we lose the contract," is a typical *either/or* statement.

Limits patterns are ways of thinking that forestall learning. Each mental pattern was based on some real experience, but as Eric Hoffer, the longshoreman philosopher, pointed out, "In a time of drastic change it is the learners who inherit the future. The learned usually find themselves equipped to live in a world that no longer exists."[1] Mental patterns that represent conclusions drawn from the past avoid new learning. They may equip you with information about what has already happened, but they open no new possibilities.

Tread Softly When Probing Limits

Directly confronting verbal limits patterns is a good way to start an unproductive argument. The limits of our maps—the borders of our belief systems, our assumptions about the world—are soft tissue and must be handled with care. Be sure that rapport exists before probing perceived limits. When your response gently poses a question that directs the discussion back toward the possibilities, you can reopen doors that have been closed. At the same time, you can find out the basis for the conclusion. Many times, when you break up the limiting pattern, the information you receive leads you to the same conclusion as the speaker. But you get there based on information, not by accepting another person's generalizations.

Exploring Boundaries with Verbal Moves

Each "limits" language pattern has a corollary probe to determine its reality base. The goal here is to determine whether the perceived limit is rooted in reality. Again, it is important to establish rapport before beginning the questioning. Those who poke roughly at the edges of our map are likely to evoke a violent reaction. Genuine concern is required. Voice tone and facial expression will give away any other mindset.

Also, we never advocate use of questions like these if they constitute a Career Limiting Move (CLM). Use good judgment to determine if probing an implied limit is dangerous, even if you are certain that the limit is not real. Assuming you have maintained rapport and are not making a CLM, here are ways to probe limits. (See Figure 9-1.)

---

[1] Eric Hoffer, *Reflections on the Human Condition* (New York: Harper & Row, 1973) 32.

The probe for a *universal* is to gently feed the key word back to the speaker as a question. "*All?*" "*Everyone?*" "Well, maybe it's just the people in accounting/marketing/R&D/operations," is a typical response. If you get a firm "Yes, *everyone* in this organization agrees on this priority," the limit may be real—if you believe the person is not mindreading, which we will get to in a moment.

When you hear an *impossible* such as "It can't be done by then," ask "*What prevents it* from being done by then?" Leave the edge out of your voice, and don't sound impatient. Follow up with a series of *specifics* questions to make sure you understand the situation.

Likewise, if you get a *necessities* response such as "*It has to be* done this way and *it must* be done by tomorrow," you can ask, "*What would happen if* it were not done this way, and it were not done tomorrow?" Of course, your tone will express concern and curiosity, not a secret conviction that their concerns are trivial.

Cause-effect is an especially good limit to probe because you are, in essence, bestowing a gift. Since the hidden limit is the belief that others can control their responses, helping people understand *they* are in charge of *their* responses can empower them. Listen to this conversation:

Jim: "*They make me* so frustrated I feel like quitting the project."

You: "*How, specifically, do they* make *you* so frustrated you feel like quitting?"

Jim: "Well, they have these useless meetings that drag on for hours where nothing ever gets done."

You: (note the use of specifics questions to explore further) "How do the meetings *make* you feel frustrated?"

Jim: "Well, maybe they don't *make* me, but I can't stand wasting time! We're under serious time pressures, and everyone sits around saying 'What if?' and not making any decisions. We've got to get rolling, or this project is dead in the water!"

You: "So your frustration is a response to the group's failure to make a decision, right?"

Jim: "Yeah!"

You: "Tell me what exactly you do to get the group to make a decision."

Jim: "What I do? Why should I do anything? Isn't it the group's job to make a decision?"

You: "The group is made up of people, and you're one of them. What prevents you from proposing that it's time to make a decision and get rolling?"

Jim: "I never thought of that. I guess I always assumed the project leader should or would do it, and got irritated when no one did. Maybe I had some choice in the matter after all. Interesting. Next time we have a meeting, I'll tell them we need to get going and watch what happens."

Notice how careful probing combines a variety of verbal moves and gives Jim options he was unaware of. Those options can empower him to get the results he wants. This does not always happen—there are plenty of real limitations out there. But in an era when resources are scarce, it is easy to fall into the trap of believing our options are scarce as well.

Mindreading is a different kind of limit. It implies that we know what goes on inside others' minds and should base our response on that. Some people verbalize their mindreading, others keep it to themselves. If not questioned, mindreading can become the accepted "reality" about someone else's thoughts and the justification for endless unproductive behavior.

Questions for responding to a *mindreading* statement such as "Management thinks we can't do the job," or "She feels they're incompetent," are *"How do you know* they think we can't do the job?" or *"How do you know* she feels they're incompetent?" Since you are after *specific* information, you can follow up with *"What specifically did you see or hear that told you* they think/she feels that way?"

Either/or is another perception about possibility. The task here is to unhook the speaker from the binary mode and get her or him to consider the existence of multiple possibilities. Hence, your response is—again, gently— *"What other possibilities might there be?"* You may hear, "There aren't any. Management says do it or else." Equally likely, however, is "I don't know. I hadn't thought about that, but maybe we *could* negotiate an extension and finish properly."

Delivery Is Everything

Subtlety is important in asking these questions. If someone says "It *has* to be done this way," your first response is likely to be a quick "What if I don't want to do it that way?" You are sending a message of defiance, not curiosity and understanding. Instead, take the position that other people's perceptions are valid, and that your job is simply to better understand them.

This is tricky when you are trying to get behind an apparent distortion of the facts. Don't get hooked on proving that what you believe is true, because others may see you as self-righteous. Only real curiosity yields learning instead of arguments. "Argue for your limitations, and sure enough, they're yours."[2] Experiment with not arguing for or against limitations; simply question them and greater possibilities will be yours.

The importance of maintaining rapport during this sort of questioning cannot be overemphasized. If you think you are losing rapport, stop probing immediately and restore the relationship before you continue. Otherwise the chances of generating major resistance skyrocket.

As you listen for these language patterns, you may hear yourself using them as well. Consider how often these limitations appear in our internal dialogue, the conversation going on inside our heads. While you recognize and probe them in others, you can do yourself the same favor!

Verification

The final aspect of getting and giving high-quality information is verification. Checking that information has been transmitted accurately is essential for every interaction. Without feeding back what you think the other person meant, you may be operating on assumptions, interpretations, and illusions—on top of the filters and limits already described!

Instead of verifying, people often fill in what they think you meant and proceed accordingly. Usually, they do not even realize they have filled in a space—they believe you provided the information they "heard." Unfortunately, the cost of those "assumptions" can be quite high in terms of wasted time, effort, and dollars.

By verifying frequently—rephrasing what you heard—you reduce the effect of your filters and transmit information with far greater accuracy. Generally, verification refers to restating what you heard using phrases such as:

Do you mean . . .?

So what you are asking me to do is . . .?

What I understood you to say is. . . . Is that right?

Let me recap what I think we've agreed to so far. . . . Do I have it?

If asking for verification seems abrupt or awkward, smooth things out with introductory statements such as "Bear with me for a moment, I want to be sure we're on track," or "Let's take a moment and review what we've cov-

---

[2] Richard Bach, *Illusions: The Adventures of a Reluctant Messiah* (New York: Delacorte Press, 1977).

ered so far." When a group appears to have reached a conclusion or changed the subject without reaching a conclusion, you may say "So are we agreed that . . .?"

Once again, make sure your voice tone and body language indicate curiosity and concern. Equally important is that you hear and use words that indicate a real understanding of the situation and what has been said. Asking if the other person understood you is NOT verification. And accepting a nod or even a verbal "Yes, I understood" without eliciting more proof of comprehension gets what you asked for; a report on the other person's confidence, not a guarantee of understanding.

If you are good at counter-examples (as in "Yes, but what about . . .?") you will, of course, think of fourteen times when you achieved good results without checking. But be honest: Weren't there as many times when it failed? Consistent verification is a hallmark of the effective professional communicator.

At first, it may feel awkward to ask for verification of understandings, agreements, and commitments. When we teach this, participants often comment that what felt to them like "over-verification" was experienced as "careful listening." Done skillfully so that it does not provoke resistance, verification quickly becomes second nature, a skill that indicates "attention to detail."

If you have taken a course in "active listening," you may recall that verifying serves other functions such as:

- Reviewing what has happened so far;
- Keeping track of where you are in a group discussion;
- Building rapport (when not overdone);
- Allowing others to feel heard; and
- Confirming plans for future action.

If you remember that it serves all these purposes and maintains the accuracy of the exchange, it is easier to verify more frequently. In fact, the habit of verification can make you enormously more effective. It will increase satisfaction in your work and reveal the remarkable number of times that another's understanding is far different from your own.

Pitfalls to Avoid

There are three pitfalls to avoid when verifying. The first is **parroting**—repeating what has been said in a mindless way that indicates you heard the words but the content never registered. Instead of building rapport, parroting quickly destroys it!

The second is **adding in elements** that did not appear in the original statements. This is tricky when you are trying to comprehend all the implications of a situation. The best thing to do is to first verify your understanding of what has already been covered, and then add "And I'm assuming this means. . . . Is that correct?" Separating the data from your interpretation of it allows you to verify both without getting caught in the "No, I didn't mean/ say that" loop.

The third pitfall is **problem-solving**. Once you confirm that you understand the situation, you can advance to problem-solving. However, combining verification and problem-solving results in lower-quality information transmission and premature solutions, cutting short "discovery" time that would yield complete understanding of the situation. People also tend to become irked when, uninvited, someone starts problem-solving their situation.

The Two-Way Street

All the skills of acquiring good information can also be used to transmit high-quality information. Your observations and rationales are far more persuasive when you provide the data that inspired them. Have you ever felt a speaker was subtly manipulating you, even though you could not put your finger on how it was happening? Frequently, you are unconsciously responding to the deletion, distortion, and generalization of base data. Technical and professional people like to make up their own minds; give them the information as well as the conclusions and you avoid triggering unnecessary resistance.

Conclusion

Language is one of our most explicit forms of behavior. Yet, compared to actual experience, it rarely seems to do what we want: reveal our world to others. The demands of the New Workplace require that we constantly bridge worlds. Understanding the built-in limitations of language permits us to bypass those limitations. By gathering additional information about the other person's experience, we create a solid and reliable basis for working together that engenders mutual understanding and mutual learning.

CHAPTER TEN

Getting Safely Out of the China Shop: How We Process Information

Phrases like "word processing," "data processing," and "information processing" are used freely in today's computer-driven world. These phrases have important equivalents on the human side. Understanding fundamentals about the way we receive and process information helps bridge gaps between people.

We have already distinguished perception from reality, and noted that each person's perceptions differ from everyone else's. We have also emphasized the value of focusing on what you *do* want rather than what you *don't* want. These insights are fundamental to the common sense syntax of skilled communicators. As you master the skills of directing attention toward certain aspects of experience, it becomes easier to recognize other differences in how other people process information. Without these insights, you are like the bull in the china shop who never quite understands why the china keeps crashing down around him.

Purpose

We will now explore even finer-grained distinctions in syntax: how the systematic ways we take in and represent information to ourselves become the media of experiencing, sharing experiences, and learning. This chapter explains how such "representational systems" operate and offers specific, systematic procedures for recognizing and working with these processing patterns. This is part of the background fabric of the Syntax Model, the context within which people can reach mutual understanding.

Representational Systems—How We Gather, Store, and Use Information

Twenty years ago, John Grinder, a linguist, and Richard Bandler, a therapist, explored and made explicit what effective communicators unconsciously know.[1] Their concept of "representational systems" was a cornerstone of the field of Neurolinguistic Programming.

That concept says that to create representations of reality, people get information by using their senses to detect signals: light, sound, movement, flavor, odor. These signals are then stored for further use. Sensory experience is stored—represented in our minds—in the form in which it is received. Each sensory input channel corresponds to an internal representational system. Thus, tastes are stored as tastes; sights as still or moving pictures; sounds as though on audio tape; tactile and emotional sensations as feelings; smells as smells.

Sensory Data—Tools for Communicating

We have all learned many tools for communication. As infants, we learn verbal and nonverbal signs and signals that allow us to express needs to our parents. Then we learn language and, within that language, we learn cultural and family variations. In school we learn standards for language as well as subtle messages about social class, region, and intellect that language conveys.

People learn these patterns, syntax upon syntax, of how to communicate, all of it rooted in sequences of sensory experience. The patterns through which we "run" sensory experiences are as powerful as the content or meaning they represent. In other words, the *way* we represent experience to ourselves is as important as *what* we think about. Those sequences are reflected in the words we choose to describe our experiences to others. The ability to hear and recognize sequences of representational systems gives us the ability to speak the "other person's language" at a very deep level.

The three most relevant representational systems are visual, auditory, and kinesthetic (both tactile and emotional sensations). Unless you are a perfume-developer or a wine-taster, modern professional life requires little ac-

---

[1] Robert Dilts, John Grinder, Richard Bandler, Leslie Cameron-Bandler, and Judith DeLozier, *Neurolinguistic Programming: The Study of the Structure of Subjective Experience,* Vol. 1 (Capitola, California: Meta Publications, 1980); Richard Bandler and John Grinder, *The Structure of Magic,* Vols. I and II (Palo Alto, California: Science and Behavior Books, 1975).

tive use of taste and smell. Dominance of representational systems depends on cultural as well as individual preferences. Cultures that place a heavy emphasis on auditory learning, such as in Muslim countries where the Koran is memorized aloud, prefer auditory systems. American culture, with its emphasis on television, is more visual.

Within those generalities, however, lie plenty of exceptions. Technical fields, for instance, in which many people, of all cultural backgrounds, prefer to work by themselves, suggest a high level of auditory processing, or internal conversation.

Actually, we *all* use *all* the representational systems all the time. The brain is constantly receiving and storing data without our awareness. That is why witnesses are sometimes hypnotized: Under hypnosis, the mind can access data collected unconsciously. And each of us prefers certain systems to take in, store, and utilize information. When information arrives in our preferred systems, we are less likely to alter it to fit our biases and unconscious filters.

Many of us assume all our representational systems have to be functioning if we are to use the one we are least conscious of. Remember the incident in the movie *Sneakers,* when the hero exclaimed, "How can we figure it out?!? I was tied up and thrown in the trunk of a car!"? The blind man then asked "What did you hear?" "I couldn't hear anything—I was tied up, hot, and uncomfortable in a pitch-black car trunk!" The hero assumed he had to have his eyes open and be comfortable to hear. The brain, however, continues to record information from all senses, regardless of whether we are conscious of it. As the scene continues, the blind man patiently extracts auditory memories of cobblestones, expansion joints on bridges, gravel roads, and, ultimately, traces the hero's course. When given the proper support, we are all capable of similar recall. For the most part, however, data is simply stored without our conscious knowledge.

Strategies

Stored sensory experiences are accessed and utilized in various combinations for specific purposes. Those combinations are called "strategies."[2] People have strategies for remembering, learning, deciding, creating, convincing, and motivating themselves. Without thinking about it, they select or attend to sensory experience in certain sequences. These sequences produce preferred and familiar results. If other people tune in and communicate in "their" sequences, they find it far easier to build mutual understanding than when sequences are extremely different.

---

[2] Dilts, op.cit.

For example, one person's buying strategy (which is actually a subset of the decision strategy) might be to see something she wants, talk to herself about whether or not to get it, go and try it out, and then listen to a voice in her head say "Yes, this is it." Someone else might first read about it (actually an auditory process—reading is auditory because written symbols represent spoken language which we learn to read by speaking the words), then go to touch and handle it, then ask others what they think, and finally get a feeling that it is the right choice. These two might have difficulty agreeing to buy the same thing at the same time.

For the most part, there are no right or wrong strategies; they are as individual as people are. Some strategies, however, are more efficient than others. For example, auditory or kinesthetic spelling (actually memory) strategies are less efficient, especially in the English language, than visual strategies. A visual memory strategy can significantly increase spelling accuracy and speed.

More helpful, however, is having multiple strategies. People who have only one strategy for making decisions, convincing themselves of something, or creating something new are less likely to function effectively in a complex world than those who have different, contextualized strategies for each activity.

Using Representational Systems

Representational systems provide one very subtle and elegant way to increase the level of rapport. Responding with language that mirrors your listener's processing patterns indicates how closely you have been listening. For example, we talked about *aligning* as a way to reduce resistance. Aligning can be performed non-verbally or verbally. If you have been listening closely, you have an opportunity to match representational systems, the sensory channels in which the person is communicating.

Thus, when you are choosing a response to a colleague who is upset with a customer, depending on his or her word choices you might consider variations like the following: "So, from your point of view, they ignored your attempts to make things clear and got exactly what they were looking for?" which is a visual match. "So it sounds to you like they're saying you're responsible for their failure to listen?" is the auditory version. "So you feel like you stepped in to help them and your efforts were rejected?" is kinesthetic.

Notice each has slightly different implications that might or might not suit the real situation. You have to pay close attention to make sure you have not aligned inaccurately. Otherwise, you will increase, not reduce, resistance.

Recognizing Your Representational System Preferences

An easy way to determine your preferred representational system is to jot down phrases that describe your last vacation (if it has been too far in the past to remember, describe your ideal vacation). Now read the lists in Figures 10-1 and 10-2 and note which phrases or words appeared in your jottings. Also notice which ones look, sound, and feel most natural; which you can imagine or remember yourself saying.

The process of creating internal representations of experience goes on at lightning-speed, well below conscious levels of thinking. Even though people may believe they reveal little about themselves in a given exchange, in fact they cannot *not* communicate. Representational system patterns are reflected by word choices and by certain aspects of behavior—breathing patterns, eye movements and body language.

Here is an example of how people reveal internal processes through word choices: "This discussion makes absolutely no sense to me; you're talking mush." This reveals a combination of auditory ("discussion") and kinesthetic ("mush") processing. A response like "I hear what you're saying; let me help you get a better handle on it" works much better than, "Let's see what I can do to show you a better picture of what this is about."

Working with Representational Systems

People with verbal variety and an ability to detect distinctions and shift easily and gracefully to someone else's preferred representational system tend to get along well with others. People who prefer to work closely with a few select peers may do so because they all have similar representational systems and strategies: that is part of what makes it easy for them to work together. It is important to recognize, however, that preferences and abilities are not always the same. Someone may be capable of great representational system flexibility and still prefer not to use it, probably because he or she is unaware of the benefits of doing so. In the New Workplace Game, this kind of flexibility is central to your effectiveness.

Whatever our processing habits, we all share one tendency, discussed in Chapter Three: to think that others experience life as we do. Not only do we think others have the same *conscious* awareness, we also assume they decide, remember, motivate themselves, learn, and create as we do.

One Syntax consultant, after listening to a speech by Winston Churchill, was convinced Churchill had a preference for visual processing—as did she.

"Predicates" are the process words and phrases used in communication. They indicate which representational system (visual, auditory, or kinesthetic) is experiencing and processing information at a given moment. Words that overlap systems or do not specifically fit in one of the three representational systems are listed as "Unspecified."

VISUAL (See)	AUDITORY (Hear)	KINESTHETIC (Feel)	UNSPECIFIED
Appear	Announce	Bearable	Analyze
Demonstrate	Articulate	Callous	Aware
Dream	Audible	Charge	Cognizant
Examine	Boisterous	Concrete	Communicate
Focus	Converse	Emotional	Conscious
Foresee	Discuss	Feel	Idea
Glance	Divulge	Firm	Intuition
Hindsight	Earshot	Foundation	Feedback
Illusion	Enunciate	Grab	Got it
Illustrate	Gossip	Grasp	Know
Image	Hear	Grip	Notice
Imagine	Hush	Handle	Perceive
Inspect	Inquire	Hang	Relate
Look	Listen	Heated	Sense
Observe	Loud	Hold	Understand
Outlook	Mention	Hunch	
Picture	Noise	Hug	
Perspective	Oral	Impact	
Proclaim	Pronounce	Lukewarm	
See	Remark	Move	
Scene	Ring	Panic	
Scope	Roar	Pressure	
Scrutinize	Say	Rush	
Show	Scream	Softly	
Sight	Shrill	Solid	
Survey	Sound	Sore	
View	Speak	Stir	
Vision	Speechless	Stress	
Watch	Squeal	Support	
Witness	Talk	Tense	
	Tell	Tied	
	Tone	Touch	
	Utter	Unbearable	
	Vocal	Upset	
	Voice	Whipped	

FIGURE 10-1: REPRESENTATIONAL SYSTEMS WORDS

The following phrases tell you how a person is experiencing and processing information.

VISUAL (See)	AUDITORY (Hear)	KINESTHETIC (Feel)
An eyeful	Blabbermouth	All washed up
Appears to me	Clear as a bell	Boils down to
Beyond a shadow	Clearly stated	Come to grips with
of a doubt	Call on	Control yourself
Bird's eye view	Discuss in detail	Cool/calm/collected
Catch a glimpse of	Earful	Firm foundation
Clear-cut	Give me your ear	Floating on a cloud
Dim view	Grant an audience	Get a handle on
Eye-to-eye	Heard voices	Get a load of this
Flashed on	Hold your tongue	Get in touch with
Get a perspective	Idle gossip	Get the drift of
on	In a manner of	Get your goat
Hazy idea	speaking	Hand-in-hand
Horse of a different	Inquire into	Hang in there
color	Keynote speaker	Heated argument
In light of	Loud and clear	Hold it
In person	Power of speech	Hold on
In view of	Purr like a kitten	Hotheaded
Looks like	Outspoken	Keep your shirt on
Make a scene	Rap session	Lay your cards on
Mental image	Rings a bell	the table
Mental picture	State your purpose	Light-headed
Mind's eye	Tattletale	Moment of panic
Naked eye	To tell the truth	Not following you
Paint a picture	Tongue-tied	Pain-in-the-neck
Photographic	Tuned in/ Tuned out	Pull some strings
memory	Unheard of	Sharp as a tack
Plainly see	Utterly	Slipped my mind
Pretty as a picture	Voice an opinion	Smooth operator
See to it	Well informed	Start from scratch
Shortsighted	Within earshot	Stiff upper lip
Show off	Word for word	Stuffed shirt
Sight for sore eyes	Sounds good to me	Topsy-turvy
Staring off into space	Clicking right along	Underhanded
Take a peek		
Tunnel vision		
Under your nose		

If you use phrases from the same representational system as the person with whom you are communicating, she or he will not have to "translate" your message and understanding will be more quickly established.

FIGURE 10-2: REPRESENTATIONAL SYSTEMS PHRASES

Upon reading the transcript, she noticed twice as many auditory words as visual ones, but she had never heard them. Auditory processing was so beyond her consciousness that she did not pick up on the words when they were spoken to her. Remember, we all operate in all systems; we have to. It is just that people screen out more in patterns that are less like their own.

There is also a category of words called "unspecified," generic words which do not specify any representational system and allow us to interpret according to our own preferences. "Truth" and "justice" are two examples. Say "justice" and one person *sees* the blindfolded goddess with her scales, another *hears* "Let he who is without sin cast the first stone," and a third person *feels* that things are fair or not. When in doubt, or when working with large groups, choosing words from all three representational systems and mixing in many unspecified words increases your chances of being understood.

Based on this introduction, concentrate on people's word choices and listen for examples from visual, auditory, kinesthetic, and unspecified representational systems. It is usually helpful to set up four columns with the headings V, A, K, and U, and sit somewhere where you can listen to conversation without participating, or listen to television or radio. Write down the words you hear in the appropriate columns. Having focused on this consciously for a while, you will find it easier to tune in to people's patterns and practice responding in matching representational systems. Even if it is not something that you work with a great deal, consider representational system processing differences as one avenue to explore if you are having trouble "getting in sync" with someone.

Conclusion

Subtle and elegant matching of representational systems is a characteristic all effective communicators have in common. You already do it much of the time, albeit not consciously. Over the next weeks and months, you will notice more and more the words people use. This increased awareness—a shift in perception—will shift your attention from content to process, from your work to the people around you. As you improve the ability to make fine distinctions and respond flexibly, you will be experienced as someone with whom it is easy to communicate. You will also be able to track how people are thinking and increase your skill at presenting your ideas in ways other people can accept. These are key skills that will increase your efficacy and enjoyment of the New Workplace Game.

CHAPTER ELEVEN

Twenty-First Century Smarts: The New Intelligence

My own, highly personal definition of what it means to be smart has changed over the years. When I was in the second grade, smart meant being able to read a word like Mississippi and then correctly announce how many syllables it had (four, right?). During my college days, smart people were the ones who wrote the most complex and amazing computer programs. Today, at college plus twenty years or so, my definition of smart means being able to deal honestly with people yet somehow avoid the twin perils of either pissing them off or committing myself to a life of indentured servitude by trying too hard to be nice.

—*Robert X. Cringely,* **Accidental Empires**[1]

Purpose

Chapter One, "The New Workplace Game," emphasized that the New Game requires significantly different skills from those formerly required of technical and other professionals. Our goal in *Smart Work* has been to present clear, precise, and useful descriptions of the behaviors that constitute those skills and let you field test them yourself. Now we revisit the concept of intelligence, or "smarts" and explore its implications. The goal is to identify and remove personal barriers that have prevented you from learning the skills of the New Game until now.

In this chapter, we enter the LEARN section of the Syntax Model and examine what enhances and constrains the learning required to play the New Game. Over the years, teaching courses in communication and effectiveness, we have wondered why one kind of behavioral learning—how to get along with people—is often so difficult for technical and other professionals: After all, they are obviously intelligent people who learn other things quite easily.

---

[1] Robert X. Cringely, *Accidental Empires: How the Boys of Silicon Valley Make Their Millions, Battle Foreign Competition and Still Can't Get a Date* (New York: Addison-Wesley, 1992).

The difficulty arises from four different areas:

- A limited view of "smarts," or the nature of intelligence;
- Learning styles;
- Interest or motivation for learning; and
- Capacity to control one's focus.

Each contributes to your interpersonal capabilities. As we examine each barrier, we will suggest ways to overcome it.

On the Subject of "Smarts"

Cringely's quote illuminates the current shift in thinking about what constitutes "smarts" in the technical world. Two scholars have done significant work in this area. One is Robert Sternberg, whose specialty is examining various forms of "practical intelligence." He defines intelligence as "the mental management of one's life in a constructive, purposeful way."[2]

Of special interest to us are certain subsets of practical intelligence: self management (e.g., ability to avoid procrastinating or losing your temper); management of others (e.g., ability to give the right job to the right person); change management (knowing how and when to adapt and when not to); and career management (ability to create and maintain a solid reputation). Practical intelligence also includes the ability to persuade, the ability to confront and collaborate, the ability to "play the game" (street smarts), and the ability to encapsulate a situation with a particularly apt metaphor or analogy. Notice in yourself which of these areas are strengths and weaknesses.

Howard Gardner's *Frames of Mind*[3] takes a different approach, delineating seven kinds of intelligence: linguistic, musical, logical-mathematical, spatial, kinesthetic, intrapersonal, and interpersonal. These are worth looking at more closely, since they help us pinpoint the strengths and weaknesses of smart technical people.

- **Linguistic (or verbal) intelligence** is the ability to convey ideas through language. This kind of intelligence can be shared by salespeople, rappers, executives, Winston Churchill, and Stephen Hawking.

---

[2] Robert Sternberg, *The Triarchic Mind: A New Theory of Human Intelligence* (New York: Penguin Books, 1988) 11.

[3] Howard Gardner, *Frames of Mind. 10th Anniversary Edition* (New York: Basic Books, 1993).

- **Musical intelligence** is the ability to appreciate and create pleasing combinations of pitch, rhythm and timbre. It functions like language, although research has placed it in another part of the brain.

- **Logical-mathematical intelligence**, also known as sequential-linear intelligence, is the capacity to abstract reality and manipulate it through long chains of reasoning to a conclusion that can then be tested. Chess players, engineers, computer programmers, financiers and research scientists have this intelligence. It is the one Cringely admired in his twenties.

- **Spatial (or visual-spatial) intelligence** is closely aligned with logical-mathematical intelligence. It is the ability to perceive the material world, transform and modify those perceptions, and create or re-create either the original or the transformed forms. Pattern recognition is part of this intelligence. People with such intelligence include engineers as well as architects, sculptors, clothing designers, and specialists in geometry.

- **Bodily-kinesthetic intelligence** is defined by Gardner as "two capacities—control of one's bodily motions and capacity to handle objects skillfully."[4] Computer keyboard skills and video games are modern expressions of this intelligence. People with this intelligence range from athletes, actors, and dancers to artisans and craftspeople, including surgeons and karate masters. Those who need to engage kinesthetically to learn are often diagnosed as learning disabled since learning institutions are usually weak in this area.

- **Intrapersonal intelligence.** Gardner discusses the personal intelligences together. He defines *intrapersonal* intelligence as "access to one's own feeling life—one's range of affects or emotions: the capacity to instantly effect discriminations among these feelings, and eventually, to label them, to enmesh them in symbolic codes, to draw upon them as a means of understanding and guiding one's behavior."[5] It is a capacity that supports poetry, journal writing, and other expressions of self-knowledge.

- **Interpersonal intelligence**, on the other hand, "turns outward, to other individuals. The core capacity here is the ability to notice and make distinctions among other individuals, and, in particular, among their moods, temperaments, motivations and intentions."[6] This is the ability of skilled diplomats, mediators, and

---

[4] Ibid., 206

[5] Ibid., 239

[6] Ibid.

process facilitators as well as political and religious leaders. It is also the kind of intelligence Cringely has come to appreciate in his middle age.

We have all of these intelligences in varying degree. Each intelligence enriches the world, and each can be enhanced through conscious effort. Groups set up to solve complex problems that include a cross-section of these capabilities are more likely to design robust solutions.[7] Of course, high-level interpersonal skills are what enable such groups to perform.

Both Sternberg and Gardner have a broader spectrum approach to intelligence than the verbal, logical, spatial definitions of traditional technical education. Whichever definition of "smart" we choose, it is clear that technical and other professional people need to expand their definition to include practical people skills. Work today demands them.

Resistance to Learning People Skills

Defining "smarts" too narrowly in technical and professional fields is only one barrier to developing "the personal intelligences." The level of interest or motivation is another. From our experience, technical and other professionals often resist interpersonal skills training. In our presentations, technical and professional audiences have given many reasons they resist this kind of learning:

- "We are strong in quantitative reasoning and critical-thinking skills, even if our interpersonal skills are weak. Most soft-skills training doesn't measure up in terms of logic and coherence. That's why we call it 'soft': It's too vague and mushy."

- "We do not have a high need for people. Satisfaction and self-esteem come from well-solved problems, not interaction with other people. What is the point in investing that kind of energy if it won't give us satisfaction?"

- "'Opportunity' comes from new and interesting problems to solve, not from getting additional people to manage. How will people skills get us more opportunities to learn? Won't they get us something we don't want instead?"

- "We are re-energized by spending time with ourselves, not with other people. People produce stress and wear. If we get good at dealing with people, we'll have to work with them more."

---

[7] Peter Kline and Bernie Saunders, *Ten Steps to a Learning Organization* (Arlington, Va.: Great Ocean Press, 1993). See "Step Five: Help People Become Resources for Each Other," 130–157.

- "Our loyalty is to our profession more than to our employers. In this era of right-sized organizations and permanent 'temporary workers,' very few organizations create the kind of institutional loyalty that leads us to place organizational needs above our own. Being good with customers may be good for the company, but we can't see what the profession—or we—get out of it."

- "For better or for worse, we know that people see us as 'different,' and sometimes we think of 'different' as 'better.' We have no desire to play stupid political games. We do *real* work."

Not only do technical and other professionals resist learning people skills, technical organizations often do not encourage it. Frequently, those who set the organizational norms perceive no need for such skills. Even when the lack of effective persuasion skills is identified as a critical factor in project failures (for example, in the tragic launch of the Challenger spacecraft), by the time the next project is on the boards everyone is again focused on the task. People skills can wait, especially under the time constraints imposed by research, prototyping, systems installations, audits or other technical work.

Learning about Your Learning Style

As discussed in Chapter Two, each of us has a personal learning syntax or style. That means each of us learns differently. When thinking about improving your learning ability, it is useful to draw a distinction between thinking and learning.[8] Learning means changing your store of knowledge, both explicit (the data you hold and its structure) and implicit (your unconscious beliefs). Thinking means working with explicit knowledge, skillfully using data in conjunction with conscious mental models and working memory.

Knowledge workers, technical and other professionals, are highly skillful thinkers. However, the traditional focus in professional learning has been too narrow. We have focused on the realm of the explicit, manipulating the data, when the New Game requires learning in the realm of the implicit, often at the unconscious levels that generate behavior. That behavior-generating level is critical to learning:

> . . . business is a dynamic process. Yet the way human cognition works, we tend to get stuck in one way of thinking. So, if you had to pick kind of an emblem of modern management, it's been 'fact-based management.' And in most cases, fact-based management is an illusion.

---

[8] Based on conversation with Mitchell Waldrop, author of *Complexity, the Emerging Science at the Edge of Order and Chaos*, September, 1992.

It's an illusion for three reasons. . . . One is that we think we under-stand the facts we have, when in fact that is quite difficult. The sec-ond is that we think we get the facts that we need. And the third is the assumption that we act on the facts. In the first one, much of what's been happening in psychological research in human cogni-tion has shown that instead of 'I'll believe it when I see it,' it's 'I'll see it when I believe it.'"

—Interview with Eileen Shapiro, author of
How Corporate Truths Become Competitive Traps.[9]

Learning at the behavior-generating level often requires a change in learn-ing style. Chris Argyris, as you may recall from Chapter Three, refers to the ability to analyze the environment and make needed external changes as "single-loop learning." This is similar to what we have just described as "thinking." "Double-loop learning" is the ability to uncover your belief sys-tems and assess their effect on your behavior in order to make changes to be more effective.[10] Because of a lack of double-loop learning, the well-trained professional who attempts fact-based analysis may run into hidden obstacles that he or she cannot even name.

For example, Argyris documented numerous examples of extremely bright consultants from major firms who lacked double-loop learning skills. They could not observe the impact of their beliefs and behavior, and change them to alter the outcome. As a result, their recommendations did not ad-dress the dynamics of belief and behavior that generated the problem in the first place. The cost, then, of "fact-based" analysis is constant bandaging rather than healing the wound.

One implication of Argyris' research is that smart people often do not know that they do not know. We often educate smart people for *content*—ex-plicit knowledge—without regard for *context*, the environment in which content operates. Yet in times of rapid change, context controls meaning. No fact is as useful alone as it is when economic, social, environmental, and political realities are factored in. That is when real learning can take place.

Context, however, can be concealed by filters, the filters described in Chap-ter Seven. This dynamic, which accounts for much of the difficulty of double-loop learning, is often described as "paradigm paralysis," the inability to see how and where the world has changed. In one fascinating study, familiar

---

[9] Tom Brown, "On the Edge: Eileen Shapiro—Some 'Truths' Won't Set You Free," *Industry Week*, 3 February, 1992.

[10] Chris Argyris, *Overcoming Organizational Barriers*, op. cit.

images were projected out of focus on a screen. Focus was sharpened in regular increments as participants tried to identify what they were seeing. The important finding was that people who guessed incorrectly at an early stage of unfocus took significantly longer to guess correctly than those who withheld judgment longer.[11] "I'll see it *when* I believe it" is exactly accurate. Once belief is established, it is a lot harder to see a situation *accurately.*

Curiosity and Courage: Roots of Learning

Two key elements enable us to see, whether or not we believe: curiosity and courage. These facilitate double-loop learning and allow us to recognize the impact of context on our results. They help us learn how to learn.

Curiosity is the driving sense of wonder that assumes there is always more to discover. It takes us beyond premature conclusions that prevent us from asking, "What other options might there be?" Curiosity around technical issues comes naturally to many of us. The task now is to take our content curiosity and apply it to context. This means redirecting curiosity to find fascinating the way each of us arrives at different views or opinions, rather than to assign blame or denigrate other paths.

There are many rewards to this shift, not the least of which is that other people begin to find *us* more interesting. That is due to the paradox that people who experience you as interested in them naturally become interested in you. Matching before you lead turns out to be a powerful learning tool!

Courage is the more difficult element of double-loop learning. People in organizations are not always encouraged to tell the truth. You may discover unpopular realities which are hard to discuss. Given that most professionals naturally fear looking, sounding, and feeling foolish, it is not surprising that so little questioning of basic assumptions (a critical piece of context) takes place, even in progressive organizations. There are many reasons to stay focused on the details—the content—rather than seek other answers for organizational breakdowns. For example, if the reward system is based on "do more of what we already do well," it takes considerable gutsiness to say "what we do no longer works." Especially after a decade of downsizing, rightsizing, mergers, and acquisitions, a job is a terrible thing to waste.

---

[11] Hyman and Anderson, as cited in William Middendorf, *What Every Engineer Should Know About Inventing* (New York: Marcell Dekker, 1981) 41.

Motivating Learning

Research on children's approaches to learning by Carol Dweck, a professor of psychology at Columbia University, holds an important key to the roots of curiosity and courage, our motivations for learning. Children who experienced their performance as proof of their ability became quickly discouraged when they ran into difficulties. They assumed that it indicated a lack of ability, which they believed to be fixed and innate. On the other hand, children who assumed that ability was incremental were challenged by difficulties and threw themselves into resolving them. They saw effort as the road to increased ability.[12]

Similarly, Robert Fritz, in his book *Creating*, suggests that adults are either performers or learners, each with a profoundly different approach to life. Performers focus on doing things well and avoiding failure. They take their natural abilities as the level of the bar, and stay close to it, in order to avoid being less than perfect. Learners focus differently: Their concern is with results, rather than performance. Hence, mistakes become feedback and they adjust to reach their goals. They fling themselves at the bar repeatedly, while raising it higher. Learners tolerate a lot of frustration, mistakes and screwups on the road to accomplishing what they want.[13]

Most people function as performers in some areas and learners in others. In terms of your people skills, where do you fall on the performer-learner continuum? Do you try and try again to communicate with people, or does one failure convince you it can not be done? Do you avoid opportunities to try new behaviors even when you know your old ones don't work? Or do you eagerly seek out opportunities to improve interpersonal effectiveness? If performance rather than learning has been your *modus operandi* in the soft skills area, what would it take to change it?

Stimulating the desire to learn, improve, and change has many roots. Do you move away from pain in response to negative prods such as being passed over for promotion, angry customer feedback or even a divorce? Or are you motivated by positive triggers such as new challenges, a colleague with especially effective interpersonal skills, becoming a parent or an experience that illuminates the power of mutual understanding? Knowing what motivates and supports your learning becomes an important tool for achieving twenty-first century smarts.

---

[12] Madeline Drexler, "Lesson Plan: Pupils View Process Differently," *Health & Fitness News Service*, 1994.

[13] Robert Fritz, *Creating* (New York: Fawcett Books, 1991).

Capacity to Control Focus

Technical and other professionals are renowned for their ability to focus and drive to completion. However, in a complex world that kind of single-minded focus cuts off an enormous amount of information, information which may be critical to our work or indicate developments that render it obsolete. Here, again, is that distinction between thinking and learning. Learning requires new information from the environment. Research on effectiveness tells us we need to maintain focus *and* respond to the environment.

It is difficult for many technical and professional people to shift attention back and forth from themselves to other people or to the environment. When paying attention to your own thoughts, opinions, or responses to another person, you are not really paying attention to anything else. Even while you tell yourself how important it is to listen, you are not listening to others because you are listening to yourself. This reminds us of the fellow who takes a lady out to dinner and talks about himself all night. When she starts yawning, he finally realizes that he has been monopolizing the conversation. His response, "Well, enough about me. Let's talk about you. What do *you* think about me?"

In reality, the issue is usually not so much overwhelming egotism as insecurity, wondering how others perceive us. Yet the end result, self-absorption, can have the same effect. Practice the skill of paying attention by listening closely to exact words and inflections, or watching for changes in facial muscles and skin color patterns. Little changes are going on all the time. Force yourself to detect them and you force your attention over to the other person.

In conversation, periodically check your responses. When someone describes an experience, do you ask further questions about the experience? Do you restate what you heard to clarify your understanding? Do you continue to listen, using silence to signal attentiveness? Or do you drift off, recalling an experience of yours that reminds you of theirs? Do you make an internal comment or judgment about the experience, or generalize about experiences of that nature? Or ask a question that *seems* to be about their experience but that actually broaches a subject you would rather discuss? All of these indicate how well you maintain and shift focus.

If you are uncertain about when to pay attention to the person and when to pay attention to the content, remember to check your goal. As long as you are moving toward it, it is safe to focus on content. At the instant the direction falters, shift back to the person and match until you can begin to move forward again.

Conclusion

Intelligence or "smarts," as currently understood, tends to describe *thinking*. It means rationalizing information from the environment into our current perceptions or paradigms, deleting, distorting or generalizing data to make them fit. If *learning* is to take place, you have to manage the issue of getting outside information to people in organizations and then being open to its meaning. Real double-loop *learning* comes from interacting with the environment.

Curiosity and courage support learning; seeing without having to believe first. They are qualities that technical and professional people have in abundance, once they decide to use them. Curiosity and courage also allow you to leverage current business trends. The changes described in the first chapters contain hidden opportunities. For instance, upper management will continue to perceive the "high-performing work team" as desirable. As a technical or professional expert, you can have a much more direct say in the development, design, and implementation of your work if you are willing to learn people skills. When you develop "twenty-first century smarts," a whole new learning curve becomes available to you.

CHAPTER TWELVE

It's Not So Hard to Learn

Learning begins when we know both our current situation and our goals. We grow when a disparity between the two activates us to move toward our goals. In that sense, learning is a generative act that requires the creation of new activity and insight.

Purpose

How can we make learning in the inter- and intrapersonal domains accessible to technical and professional individuals? Increase your aptitude for double-loop learning and significantly increase your effectiveness in the New Game? While we have discussed many aspects of your personal learning strategy, or syntax, in previous chapters, here we will look at the learning process generically and complete our discussion of the LEARN element of the Syntax Model. The previous chapter explored barriers to learning. This chapter covers theory about how people learn; discusses perception, choice, and self-sabotage; and offers suggestions for building support within your organization for people skills learning.

Why Learn People Skills?

We need to engage our resources and talents to respond to the new order of challenges faced by individuals, organizations, and society—the "New Rules for the New Workplace" described in Chapter Two. Complex times demand new ways to perceive, decide what matters, and organize ourselves. These new ways fall into the realm of what has been called "personal mastery, the discipline of continually clarifying and deepening our personal vision, of focusing our energies, of developing patience, and of seeing reality objectively."[1]

To achieve personal mastery, you need to become an observer of your own internal processes; to that end you need frameworks to make sense of those processes. You must move from traditional passive learning to generative,

---

[1] Peter Senge, *The Fifth Discipline* (New York: Doubleday, 1990) 7.

interactive, double-loop learning. Technical and professional people, as much as anyone, need to be part of this shift from thinking to learning. Because your knowledge and expertise are at the very core of what is now possible, you are instrumental to effecting changes in society.

Learning How to Learn for Personal Mastery

There is no stronger catalyst to learning than curiosity. Curiosity without judgment has been called learning at its best. It is the learning that absorbs the whole picture through play and exploration. As children, our goal was to know more; we asked about everything and "Why'd" our parents to distraction. As we grew older and went to school, we experienced "hardening of the paradigms"—learning that there was *one* right answer, *one* right way to do things. Performance and analytical thinking were emphasized; we were taught to judge and evaluate. As a result, much of our creativity and openness to possibility was lost.

Just as brainstorming works best when we do not evaluate, we learn best when we remove judgments about performance. Current research on how the brain works indicates that learning to play reopens our brains. It is not that play is good and analysis bad; what is important is the sequencing. Play first and analysis afterward allows us to come up with creative ideas and explore multiple understandings before we narrow the options. For many, mastering this process requires a significant amount of *un*learning, a deliberate letting go of old ways.

Feedback also strongly enhances personal mastery, supplying useful information about reality. Not surprisingly, people who need greater intra- or interpersonal intelligence tend to be unaware of or indifferent to their deficiencies. Feedback about such weaknesses may fall on deaf ears. Videotaped presentations, role plays, or group interactions can create feedback powerful enough to break through to such people. Video can be the bridge from "seen when believed," as Shapiro puts it, to "believed when seen." Please note that sometimes this kind of feedback is so overwhelming that the recipient needs to be in a safe and supportive environment to receive it.

Another way to make progress towards personal mastery is through personal growth experiences. Personal growth experiences range from programs like Outward Bound and Forum or Lifespring to twelve-step programs and in-depth therapy. Addressing deep emotional issues requires the assistance of someone trained to respond in useful ways. Each individual chooses the form that is most appropriate. People usually feel more comfortable disclosing personal issues outside the work environment. The common goal is a renewed recognition of strengths and resources, along with understanding that you are not the only one with limiting or embarrassing weaknesses.

The Law of Requisite Variety

Effective professional performance entails operating as a part of a system. Human communication, like communication technology, exists within a system; relevance, value, and meaning derive from interaction with other parts of the system. One human being sitting on a rock talking to him or herself is not communication! The only part of a shared communication system any one can control, however, is his or her own input. Becoming a professional communicator, as we discussed in Chapter Six, means understanding that *if what I do does not produce the results I desire, I must do something differently.* Cybernetics, the study of neurological and automated systems controls, has a rule for systems behavior, the Law of Requisite Variety[2], which says that *the element in the system with the most flexibility ultimately gains the most control within the system.*

Notice that this does not say gains *complete* control. Notice also that it is a long-term approach. Bullies often do get their way, short-term. Long-term, those with higher-order communication skills—and well-focused personal goals—are more likely to succeed.

When the film director Steven Spielberg was a child, he was unmercifully bullied by a larger classmate. Upon receiving his first Super-8 camera for his twelfth birthday, he sought out the bully and asked him to be the action hero in a movie. Amazed, the bully at first assumed Spielberg was making fun of him. Spielberg persisted, and the bully starred in several of his high school films, becoming Spielberg's good friend (and personal bodyguard) throughout high school. Spielberg's unexpected response to the bully is excellent proof of the Law of Requisite Variety.

One of the goals, then, of new behavioral learning is to increase your Requisite Variety. Increased behavioral variety extends your sense of play, your ability to respond creatively to seemingly hopeless situations, and your influence in the New Workplace. These are compelling reasons for putting more conscious effort than ever into *learning how to learn,* as well as into learning how to behave skillfully with others. Now let's turn our attention to the learning process itself, to make it easier to manage.

---

[2] W. Ashby, *An Introduction to Cybernetics* (London, England: Chapman and Hall Ltd., 1956).

Steps in Learning

People go through four steps in learning, as illustrated in Figure 12-1.

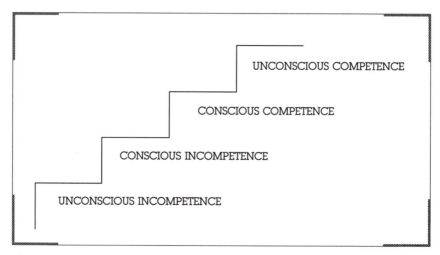

FIGURE 12-1: STEPS IN LEARNING

Start at the bottom. Remember when you were a kid and had never seen a computer? You did not know they existed, and you could not work them, but that didn't matter since you were totally unaware of them. This is *unconscious incompetence*. You didn't know you didn't know.

Later, you encountered a computer and were intrigued: "How do you get it to work?" you wondered. This is the stage of *conscious incompetence*, where you were aware of computers but knew you could not operate one. Now, you knew you didn't know.

After a while, the mysteries of UNIX, DOS, and PASCAL began to unravel. With much concentration and effort, you made your way through the system, maybe even wrote and debugged a program of your own. At this point you had reached *conscious competence:* You could do it *if* you paid attention. You knew you knew.

Finally, you stopped needing to pay attention. The computer became an extension of your thoughts and hands. It was a tool for getting things done, not something you had to pay attention to in and of itself. You had attained *unconscious competence!* You didn't know you knew.

Your learning of interpersonal behaviors very likely followed a similar path. Since it happened when you were quite young, however, the moment of "conscious competence" was both brief and barely conscious: "Oh, that doesn't work any more," you concluded as your parents failed to respond to your temper tantrum or "Hmm, saying 'please' seems to get me what I want more often."

One thrust of *Smart Work* is to usher you to "the observation deck." You are now aware of, and can observe, your behavior from the outside. Paying close attention to your own behavior enables you to pinpoint moments of conscious competence. Those are the moments when choice first appears, the moments at which you can generate more options for the future.

Comfort and Safety

Remember this about the learning progression: Conscious competence may not feel comfortable. Whether you reach it from the step below en route to mastering a new skill, or from above by teaching something you already know very well, this stage is not as easy as the others. Try this experiment: Cross your arms over your chest the way you normally would. Now reverse them. Notice how strange and "not right" that unimportant change in behavior feels. Of course, learning something new feels even more uncomfortable.

Real learning, the kind that produces implicit knowledge (see Chapter Eleven) does not occur when people feel totally comfortable. Notice the important distinction between safety and comfort. People need to feel *safe* to learn; but they do not need to feel *comfortable*. Once again, much depends on where you focus your attention. If you are caught up in the learning process, fascinated by what you are learning, and eager to learn more, you are unlikely to notice the discomfort. If you actively resist, however, the discomfort may be the only thing you think about.

We have written *Smart Work* well aware of the potential discomfort of learning new behavior. We sometimes go out on a limb or attempt to deliberately provoke. We hope this material shakes you out of your comfort zone once in a while. There is also a high degree of safety here, both in the exercises and in your use of Syntax skills. More than a decade of working with these tools and techniques tells us they will work with a minimum of toxic side effects. More importantly, you *already* use them to some extent, and you deserve the benefits of elevating them to "conscious competence."

Steps in Development

Flexibility in communication means having a wide range of behavioral options. Changing behavior, especially at the "default" level, can be a long, slow process. Since *you* are the part of the communication system you can control, move yourself to the observation deck, examining each situation to find out where your behavior produces unsatisfactory results. Then, depending on your learning style, you may either make steady incremental progress at practicing new behaviors or go for a long time with no change and suddenly integrate several new behaviors at once. There is no right or wrong. It is another instance where knowing your style helps you be more tolerant of your change process.

Meanwhile, it helps to know that, just as learning and professional development proceed in a logical progression, there is a progression toward behavioral learning. Take the following steps toward improved communication:

1. From the observation deck, notice the results of poor communication, results that are markedly different from what you intended.

2. Identify the poor communication behaviors: What, specifically, did you do?

3. Notice yourself performing the behavior; become aware of what you are doing *while* you are doing it.

4. Recognize the behavior at the moment it starts, not once you're doing it or when it's over. You still cannot stop, but at least you know when you are about to do it.

5. Finally, recognize you have a moment of choice: You can repeat your old unsuccessful behavior, or you can *do something different.*

This moment of choice is crucial. If you never recognize that you have a choice, if you do not understand that you can do something different *at this instant,* then you never have the opportunity to elicit different results. In human affairs, *if you always do what you have always done, you will always get what you have always gotten.* If your results please you, do not change. If they don't please you, then you need moments of choice to recognize opportunities to act differently.

It is hard for most of us to do something different without a clear sense of what it might be. You have been introduced to dozens of possible moves in the preceding chapters. We do not assume that you will run out and instantly use all our suggestions. One or two will seem immediately applicable; many more should be saved for the moment of need. Trust that you will have them when you need them, and then review **Smart Work** from time to time to refresh your unconscious and conscious memory.

Self-Sabotage Prevention: The Value of the Model

Each of us has ways of sabotaging our results. We may lack focus and muddle along unclear about what we desire. We may have friction in communicating with others, making ourselves unpromotable due to "personality conflicts" and "inability to get along with others."

For others, self-sabotage might mean not getting information right: either getting insufficient information, not getting the right level of detail, distorting or forgetting information we have received, or not knowing how to figure out what we need to know. And, certainly, many of us lose ground by defending our actions, rather than learning from experience. When we justify doing things the way we have always done them and screen out feedback, we ignore data that would increase interpersonal effectiveness.

Almost everyone relies on mechanisms—reminder cards or feedback or additional training or other kinds of reinforcement—to strengthen areas of weakness or change old behavior patterns. Our unconscious self-sabotage loops often undermine such carefully chosen cures. The value of an external reference such as the Syntax Model, like all good maps, is to give you your bearings when you feel lost or disoriented. It reminds you of the syntax, or pattern of behavior, that will route you directly back to where you want to go. Focus or results orientation may be your strong suit, or flexibility may be your best skill. Balancing the two dynamics overcomes most self-sabotaging tendencies.

What Learning Gets You

Ultimately, learning generates more choices. The following case study comes from a Harvard Business School study of two-person relationships.[3] As you read it, keep in mind the concepts of single-loop (data-analysis) and double-loop (analysis at the level of beliefs that generate behavior) learning.

Tom, a vice president of sales, had nurtured the career of Steve, his sales manager, and considered him one of the best in the company. When Tom was asked to recommend someone to turn around the marketing services department, Steve's name came immediately to mind. He sent Steve a message asking him to come in and discuss it. It was a sign that his division was in good shape that Tom could think about letting Steve go. He also

---

[3] John J. Gabarro and Eileen Morley, "Understanding Two-Person Relationships," *Harvard Business School Case Studies.*

thought Steve was strong enough to turn around the perception of marketing services as a repository for employees who had ceased to be effective in the field. The position would also give Steve exposure and influence at the corporate level.

During a surprisingly distant conversation in which Steve seemed ill at ease, Tom explained why he thought Steve could handle the job. Tom suggested that Steve call the marketing vice president to discuss it. About a month later, Steve's area manager called to say that Steve had left the company to go with a competitor. Tom later found out that Steve had left because he believed he must have been considered ineffective if he was to be sent to marketing services. Both had reason to believe their positions made sense.

Steve's behavior exemplifies the danger of single-loop learning. There was nothing wrong with his (single-loop) analysis at all. Inability to consider the possibility that the underlying assumptions might not be correct (double-loop learning) produced distress and ultimately forced a job change. Similarly, Tom's inability to consider how things might look from Steve's point of view, given marketing services' image, generated negative dynamics.

The outcome might have been different had either one asked a few hard questions. Steve: "What's going on? We both know that department has always been for losers, and I don't think I deserve that." Or Tom: "Steve, I'm offering you a major promotion. What exactly is getting in the way of your taking it?" Because of unconscious assumptions, Steve and Tom lost the opportunity to make important conscious choices.

The incidence of misunderstanding and single-loop learning can be reduced by consistent attention to the way you communicate in day-to-day situations. It is even more effective to use a reference system such as the Syntax of Effectiveness. Then, as you observe repetitive patterns or levels of ineffectiveness that hamper coordinated action, you can analyze them quickly and in depth by reviewing the parts of the Model. Once you have identified the weak spot—failure to link adequately, lack of sufficient information, lack of a clear goal, overlooking the results that specific behavior is generating—it is relatively easy to bring the process back into alignment.

Strategies for Getting Support

Once *you* are convinced, how do you get managers to realize that quality technical work in the New Game requires extensive "soft" skills training that produces real behavior change? Ed Brady, senior vice president and general manager of the MITRE C³1 division, reported that it took seven years for middle managers who received such training to progress to upper management, where they required it of everyone. A global manufacturer of energy projects found that it took three and a half years *and two and a half changes in management* to complete the cultural change from energy equipment sales (technical-skills intensive) to energy services (people-skills intensive). "People never get fired here because of their technical skills," the general manager noted. "Heads roll because of a lack of people skills. And they never see it coming."

So how *do* you convince them? Start by asking questions: "Does this 'soft stuff' matter?" "How?" Then draw attention to the costs of redoing a project because the need was poorly defined the first time. Observe aloud the time wasted when workers make wrong decisions because they do not develop a shared vision of the end result early on. Calculate how much time is wasted in meetings with no clear goal and in meetings where people sit around blaming each other instead of figuring out how it could be different. Pinpoint how the team's failure to build rapport with other groups costs it dearly when it needs their cooperation.

While this is going on, research the benefits of soft skills training. Read how trained facilitators at Ford—ordinary people like you—have been a major factor in its turnaround. Note that most Baldrige National Quality Award winners have undergone intensive training in communication skills and team and group dynamics. And point out to your managers and peers that the Japanese (and many other cultures) receive lifelong education in paying attention to other people's responses, training which is almost totally lacking in our culture.

Another approach is to benchmark. Ask, "Who is the best in the field?" "Who is particularly successful right now?" And then ask, "How much 'soft side' training is that organization doing?" Very often, you will discover major training commitments in general and high levels of interpersonal skills training in particular.

The ultimate strategy for obtaining support will be to put the burden back where it belongs. Most technical education was designed in the '50s and has not changed substantially since. Many other forms of professional training use the same model. Our education produced or reinforced our narrow focus. Now higher education must teach that technical skills alone are no longer enough and require other kinds of skills as well for graduation or certification. It is a new world and a new workplace, and our past education processes served us poorly in preparing for this world. We can no longer afford the luxury of a narrow focus on explicit knowledge. We all have to pay attention to the big picture and the bottom line.

Conclusion

Each of us has a personal learning syntax. There are learning dynamics at work in every situation that transcend that syntax, such as the steps in learning. Getting up to your observation deck to review your goals and how you achieved them extracts learning from every interaction and counteracts self-sabotage. Consider the potential benefits of alerting your organization to the growing need for new kinds of learning and new behavioral norms. Remember that curiosity is the key. Avoid self-condemnation. In learning, *there is no failure, only feedback.*

CHAPTER THIRTEEN

Requests and Agreements

To become conscious of patterns of behavior, recognize the here-and-now choices, and accumulate a wide repertoire of useful actions are reasons for reading *Smart Work*. Throughout the book, we have treated language as a reflector of experience, the surface statement of a rich experience base. Now we want to explore it in a different way; language as action. We will examine it as a set of interactive "moves," not as an encoding of information. Once again, we will observe the fundamental patterns of our personal syntax, this time looking at how we ask and give and agree and renegotiate.

Purpose

All the aspects of the Syntax Model of Effectiveness that we have discussed so far prepare you for the next and most powerful step in refining the ways you communicate. The information in this chapter enables you to work out most of the knots in interpersonal communication by providing the tools for saying "I want or need this," or "Yes," or "No." These are the tools of effective requests and agreements. They provide the central balancing mechanism of the Model. The chapter outlines ways to use requests and agreements to maintain balance in a complex world. They enable *you* to recognize and choose what you will and will not do, communicating your choices in ways that maintain good working relationships and appropriate boundaries.

Narrowed Choices

Requests and agreements, called "conversational moves" by Fernando Flores,[1] reflect how you decide and agree to work. As a result of cultural and family patterns, you have learned to narrow your choices in getting what you want and meeting the needs of others. The goal now is to restore a wider range of choices by developing conscious awareness of these patterns.

---

[1] Terry Winograd and Fernando Flores, *Understanding Computers and Cognition: A New Foundation for Design* (Menlo Park: Addison-Wesley, 1987) Chapter 11.

Eric Berne, founder of Transactional Analysis, described such patterns in his 1962 book *Games People Play.*[2] Berne noted sequences of behaviors that serve to keep us in pre-chosen life roles. These patterns represent a large element of our personal syntax, a set of moves learned as we grew up. They also reflect decisions about how to operate within the context of our families and schools. How we ask and agree with others is a profound expression of these early decisions; how we adjust those behaviors in adult life is the key to realizing forgotten possibilities. Once again, effort is required to learn new patterns, and the payoff can be dramatic.

Keeping Agreements

Having observed the patterns in personal syntax through the lens of agreements, we believe *life works much better when you keep your agreements.* Many people agree with this and sincerely want to keep their agreements. Still, they somehow make agreements that do not work for them and then fail repeatedly to fulfill or renegotiate them.

If you reflect on transactions within your organization, you can probably recall numerous occasions when trust was broken, resentment created, or projects trashed because agreements were broken. Perhaps people believed they had no choice when they made the agreements, or they did not know when or how to renegotiate the agreement, or they truly did not understand what they agreed to.

Training in the process of making agreements is often framed as negotiation skills, and includes strategies and techniques for gaining the upper hand. When you approach a situation assuming that there are one-up and one-down positions to be held, you are likely to reinforce that belief and make the situation more difficult than it really is. Given the central role agreements play in getting anything done, it is disturbing that "common sense" still perpetuates such unproductive beliefs and methods.

As we step through the structure of conversations that lead to successful agreements, we will also comment on the limiting beliefs or habits that get in the way. Take time to observe your habitual way of making agreements and you will find valuable ways to reduce confusion and needless conflict.

Radical Shifts

You may assume that by taking a job, you renounce your right to say "yes" or "no." Learning to take charge of requests and agreements is a radical

---

[2] Eric Berne, *Games People Play* (New York: Grove Press, 1962).

thing to do. It may not be easy. It provides no greater control over other people's behavior than anything else, but it does help you do your best to make your requests and intentions understood. Through the ripple effect, your behavior creates an environment where others clarify their choices.

When a human resource professional from Spain joined our group of consultants, we introduced her to the model of requests and agreements. She easily grasped the structure of complete requests and how to give a simple "yes" or "no." But when she tried to say "no," especially to someone she perceived as having more power in the situation, she was *physically* unable to get the word out of her mouth. She was overwhelmed by the flood of feelings and inner messages triggered by that action.

In Spain, as in every culture, there are hundreds of ways to imply "no" and hundreds of situations where it is unthinkable to say the word directly. In every country that we know of, people put up with what they do not want and experience major distress if they try to break the pattern. This is also true in every organization we know of.

Requests and Work

In writing about setting goals in Chapter Five, we cited requests as the starting point for doing work. As the balance point in the center of the Syntax Model, requests work best once you know your desired outcome (PLAN) and have established rapport (LINK). Knowing which requests are appropriate comes from skillful information gathering (INFORM). Making the requests produces action with observable results (LEARN).

Clarity and completeness in making requests leads to productive work and satisfied customers. Think about your organization. Who requests your work? Whose work is a response to your requests? How does this serve as a basis for determining your effectiveness in terms of productivity and customer satisfaction?

Requests, as a class of ways to reveal your wishes, express various levels of urgency and authority. For example, a *command* implies that the requester has authority over the listener. An *invitation* implies that acceptance is up to the listener. A *plea* suggests that the listener has more authority than the requester. A *demand* may or may not be backed with power, but it is heard as urgent.

There are many forms of requests. How do we know one when we hear one? One simple definition is that a request is made when a listener understands what the requester wants. This can happen even when the requester uses non-verbal communication or verbal shorthand to express the request.

The listener's understanding is the basis for coordinated action, a clear-cut example of the saying, "The meaning of your communication is the response you get."

What Is an Agreement?

An agreement is made when the listener promises to do what the requester asks. The requester has a future action in mind. How well the listener performs the action depends on how well the requester has communicated and the extent of the listener's ability and willingness. When the action has been performed and reported to the requester, the agreement has been completed. If it gets performed but not reported, the agreement is not really completed. In day-to-day work, much frustration and resentment can be traced to breakdowns occurring at points throughout the process.

New Choices

There are many effective ways to make requests and agreements. Organizations and groups have their own customs about making requests and agreements, and about who makes requests of whom. Close attention to the structure of requests cuts through defensive routines and confusion and corrects breakdowns. Be gentle; people want things to stay as they are even when you are certain that greater effectiveness is only a conversational move away.

Observing your own patterns of requests and responses requires time on the observation deck. It gives you perspective on how you obtain what you want and need, and how you respond to what others want and need. Once you observe your patterns, you may find that you overlook some choices or omit important elements.

Structure, Not Formula

Consumer Protection Warning: You cannot learn this structure of requests and apply it as a formula, a tool for always getting the "right answer." That idea ignores the flow of situations, as well as the fluency that characterizes the successful requester. It is a dance. The best dancers can dance with good partners and less skillful ones. Anyone who tries to do it by the numbers or follow the footprints pasted on the floor is going to have a tough time. Follow the footprints for a while, then let go and get into the swing. Find a few good partners with whom to practice your new moves.

Requester and Listener

Let's review the structure of successful requests. First, the requester has to make clear who is asking and who is being asked. This seems obvious. In fact, this whole structure seems obvious when you focus attention on it. So why do we consistently use less-than-effective patterns in our personal syntax? Possibly because we are committed to acting out early decisions about ourselves: "People won't want to do what I want them to." "I have to go underground. I'll only get part of what I want anyway, but at least I'll get something." "I don't dare ask this person to do something for *me*."

The result is requests in which who asks and who is asked are often strangely missing. You have heard this pattern many times: "The kitchen/ your room/the garage needs cleaning." "The dog needs to be walked." "The decision needs to be made." Who is asking whom? Who "owns" this situation? *You*, if it is something *you* want. Or it may be you as a representative of someone else, such as people in your work group, a customer, or your manager.

Structure of a complete request:

- Requester: Who is asking?
- Listener: Who is being asked?
- Future Action: What do I want you to do?
- Conditions of Satisfaction: How will I know it's been done?
- Time: By when?

This structure is present in effective requests, although they may not always be spoken. What is relevant is what was received, as demonstrated by the response of the listener.

Related actions:

- Make offer
- Request clarification
- Report completion

FIGURE 13-1: MAKING COMPLETE REQUESTS

Wherever possible, select someone to ask who is capable of fulfilling your request. Requests directed to no one in particular or to someone unable to fulfill them produce a surprising proportion of human frustration. In many organizations getting access to the right listener is most of the work involved in making a request. Stop and think through who should be asking and who should be asked before you put your request out there.

Future Action

The next part is to say *what* you want. Most likely it is an action to be taken, something you want done. What actions do you request most often at work? What actions have been requested of you? Listen closely to how people specify what they want done. It is interesting to study the less-than-precise exchanges that take place every day at work. When preparing a request, be clear on the action you want taken.

Conditions of Satisfaction

Next, you need to specify *how* you want it done, your *conditions of satisfaction*. If you do not specify your conditions as you make a request, you end up taking pot luck. Life will give you plenty of that, without your asking. It is up to you, when you want something, to define it clearly enough to enable the listener to satisfy you.

The concept of conditions of satisfaction, however, makes a powerful assumption: that you *can* be satisfied. How willing are you to actually get what you want? Do you believe the world is a place where there is enough to go around, and that it is OK for you to be satisfied? Have you reflected on this recently? If you have not thought much about these issues (and most people have not), this is a potent opportunity.

Specify your conditions of satisfaction. Do it in the context of goals, rapport, clear information, and the Aim Frame (what you do want rather than what you don't). Then observe the shifts in the results you get. The ability to maintain this focus and flexibility on a daily basis makes you both effective and easy to work with, the keys to success in the New Workplace Game.

Time

Time is the last element of a request, and an important one: When do you want this done? More assumptions are made about this element than any other. You may specify the nature of the request and the conditions of satisfaction to a listener capable of performing the request, but then fail to say when you need the job done.

One person may hear an urgent need as a casual request, or the other way around. A manager may express a whim, and a staff that wants to please him devotes much more time and energy to the task than the manager would want.

One newly promoted vice president of a large corporation commented on the ugly colors of the chairs in the company cafeteria. A week later he noticed they had been changed. "That's great! Who requested the change?" he inquired. "You did, sir," came the response. Requesting clarification, such as asking "When, specifically, do you need this?" is essential for clear requests and agreements.

Direct Requests

- I ask that you . . .
- I request . . .
- Will you . . .?
- Do this.

Common (Less Effective) Forms of Request

- I want or I need . . .
- Why don't you . . .?
- _____ needs to be done.
- Can you . . .?
- Would you mind . . .?

FIGURE 13-2: EXAMPLES OF REQUESTS

The Language of Requests

The most effective requests use language as action. For example, by saying "I ask that you . . ." or "I request . . ." you are not merely presenting your experience through choice of words. You are, instead, _doing_ what it is you say you are doing, in real time; you are asking. The words are the action. Effective requests combine the needed level of detail with action language.

Less effective requests either leave out essential detail or don't actually *ask;* they make statements but don't perform the action of asking. Here are examples:

- *Effective request:* "I ask that you, Jerry, finish costing out this proposal by June 8. I want the total costs of equipment, time, travel, and supplies, with quotes from the vendors, on my desk by noon of that day."
- *Less effective request:* "I need to have your proposal finished the first week in June."

Think about the kind of language you normally use for requests. What could you do to make them more effective immediately?

Responses to Requests

How much choice you have about doing what others ask of you (or what you think they are asking) is reflected by your response. Remember the song "I'm Just a Girl Who Can't Say No," from the musical *Oklahoma?* More people than you think are like that! There is also "I'm just a person who can't say yes." Most people's personal syntax is sadly deficient in its range of responses to requests.

If you can't say "no," you probably can't really say "yes" either. Think about it. Exercising your full range of options is empowering. You become accountable for your responsiveness to others; you no longer accept false responsibility or indulge in passive escapism. Effective requests and agreements maintain balance between yourself and others. If you feel like you have a choice, you are much more likely to do what you say you will do.

The choice of responses, with examples, are shown in Figure 13-3 on the next page.

After reviewing the responses, which do you find easiest to use and which are most difficult? The ability to decline is an important key to staying in balance. Discussing it is one thing, doing it, as mentioned before, is quite another. Spend a few moments on the observation deck reviewing all the ways you said "no" today. Were there situations where you wish you had said "no" but didn't? Become an observer of what happened instead, and notice whether you are willing to give yourself more choices. Practice "No, that doesn't work for me," several times, then try it out in a real situation. If you are someone who is clear on "yes" and "no" much of the time—congratulations! It is so much better to live and work around people who are willing to say what they want and don't want, and work out the difference constructively.

Some of the responses in the table may not have occurred to you, such as saying, "I'll tell you later," (commit to commit) instead of responding right away. Counteroffers are also an important part of reaching agreement and, surprisingly often, a series of counteroffers leads to a more mutually satisfactory agreement than either person would have requested alone.

- **Promise**: Agree, Yes, I'll do it.
- **Decline**: No, I promise not to do it.
- **Counteroffer**: I won't do that, and I offer this instead.
- **Commit to Commit**: I will let you know after . . .
- **Renegotiate**: As soon as I know that I won't keep our agreement, I'll let you know and do what I can to make up the difference.

Examples of Responses

Promise
- I agree to . . .
- Yes, sure, ok.
- That works for me.

Decline
- No.
- No, thank you.
- That doesn't work for me.

Counteroffer
- I can't do X. How about Y instead?
- Would Y be an acceptable alternative?

Commit to commit
- I'll let you know after I check with . . .
- I'll think it over and get back to you by . . .

Renegotiate
- I said I would do X, and now I realize I won't be able to. What can I do to help you find another way?

FIGURE 13-3: RESPONSES TO REQUESTS

Sometimes You Renegotiate

Have you been in a situation where you knew you could not fulfill an agreement you had made but did not tell the other person right away? Many people find renegotiation uncomfortable and put it off. The longer you put off renegotiating your agreement, the more inconvenience you create for the other person. Renegotiating takes not only courage, but also skill. Telling someone, "I said I could do this but I can't; how can I help you handle it now?" early on will earn a lot more respect than last-minute excuses. When human beings make agreements they usually mean to keep them. Since circumstances often change, we need to give ourselves and others the room to renegotiate.

Do "Field Study"

You may find it intimidating or upsetting to become conscious of these patterns. You may not be happy about how you handle requests and agreements. Before deciding to change anything, go to the observation deck. Do field study. Raising the issue in your work environment can be risky because it pinpoints the sloppy way work gets requested, agreed to, done, delivered, and evaluated. Nonetheless, you can gain considerable leverage by learning to employ the structure of effective requests and agreements. And considerable relief from improving situations that don't make sense now.

Conclusion

This is powerful material. Requests and agreements govern much of our daily lives. Think about the people with whom you coordinate action, starting with your household and co-workers. They are your real-world lab. We have introduced the elements to observe, and pointed out the depth of habit and custom at work. Practicing these skills and adding this balance mechanism to your existing skills of clarity and communication can create major breakthroughs in mutual understanding.

CHAPTER FOURTEEN

Teamwork's Underlying Structure

Teamwork is where the rubber meets the road in inter- and intrapersonal learning. Teams *are* the New Workplace, living laboratories that provide ongoing opportunities for you to get up on the observation deck and perform systematic field study. You see your personal syntax in action over and over again, at the same time you observe other people's. The issue of choice is distilled in the pressure cooker of the team environment through the constant interplay of behavioral patterns. Do you choose your responses? Or do you let team dynamics choose them for you? The decision is yours to make.

Purpose

We have described actions for building links with colleagues, managing information flow, and moving work along through requests and agreements. We have now reached the application stage of the learning process. Teams provide the perfect context for employing the behaviors we have introduced.

Let's step back and take another look at underlying dynamics—in this case, the dynamics of teams. This chapter presents a simple framework for recognizing these dynamics and points out which Syntax skills will help you work through every stage of team growth and development.

The Syntax of Group Behavior

In most professional fields, robustness is crucial in the design of good systems. Robust systems are strong and vigorous, able to withstand a wide range of adverse conditions, and still function well. Groups working together need to develop similar robustness—to work well together during all stages of a project and under a variety of pressures and constraints. Robustness can be developed if you understand the underlying dynamics of groups.

The behavior of individuals in groups has been studied for several decades. All groups, especially those assigned to perform specific tasks, go through distinct behavioral stages. These stages are the natural products of basic human needs—for security, for identity, for stimulation, for connection, for accomplishment, and for control. Groups that accomplish a lot over an extended period of time are groups that meet all members' needs. Groups that work well together on shorter projects do so because a natural fit of personality types fulfills those needs, or because members of the group use their awareness of group dynamics to smooth the way. In either case, dynamics determine the effectiveness of the team. They are the underlying structure of group behavior—its syntax.

As you can see in Figure 14-1, syntax operates in two fields: the group's *content* (the work assigned and the goal of that work) and its *process* (how it does that work). The process aspect contains two key areas: task and maintenance. The task element corresponds to the FOCUS axis of the Syntax model; it is about setting goals and learning how to accomplish them to get the job done. The maintenance element corresponds to the FLEXIBILITY axis—it is about relationships in the group, how members maintain rapport, handle resistance, and circulate information. The actions described in *Smart Work* are powerful aids to developing and maintaining positive, productive, and enjoyable group dynamics in both areas of the process aspect.

CONTENT—the purpose the group serves

PROCESS—how it achieves that purpose

- **Task**—how it does the work

- **Maintenance**—how it manages relationships

FIGURE 14-1: SYNTAX OF GROUP WORK

At the same time that the syntax of the group's work is operating, a syntax of relationships develops within the group. Depending on the purpose of the group the dynamics may vary, but there are almost always four basic stages of group development. These are illustrated by Figure 14-2, based on the work of Bruce Tuckman.[1]

FORMING—polite introductions, members size each other up

STORMING—struggle to establish power relations

NORMING—members' roles are agreed upon

PERFORMING—real work gets accomplished

FIGURE 14-2: TUCKMAN'S STAGES OF GROUP DEVELOPMENT

Forming

The first stage of any group process is exploratory, each individual wondering, "Who am I in this group?" "How will they treat me?" "How should I act?" "Do I belong in this group?" "Is anyone going to take control from me?" "How can I maximize control over what happens to me?" Feeling wary and cautious, members are busy presenting credentials and sizing each other up. On the surface, there is cool politeness: "So nice to meet you, I've heard so much about your work." Members fall into observer roles and wait for someone else to make the first move. Tuckman called this the *forming* stage.

As the leader, allowing time for people to introduce themselves and get to know each other at the beginning sets a tone that says, "People will be important in this process. *You* will be important." This allows people to hold their control issues a little more lightly. For all members, forming is

---

[1] Adapted from Bruce W. Tuckman, "Developmental Sequence in Small Groups," *Psychological Bulletin,* Vol. 63, 1965.

the stage at which to employ rapport-building skills. Using all the information received through word choices, representational systems, language patterns, and non-verbal behavior, you can practice matching at multiple levels. This, in turn, sends messages about who you are that positively affect subsequent stages of group dynamics. It allows you to pay close attention to others' behaviors and needs. It also allows you to minimize "What kind of impression am I making?" and other anxiety-provoking internal questions.

Storming

The next stage of group development is the process of developing ownership and leadership. It is usually met with resistance. "Wait a minute, nobody elected you king (or queen)!" "Who appointed you God?" "No way I'm going to let that guy take control over my work," and similar thoughts come to mind as soon as someone starts to set the agenda. Depending on people's temperaments and the circumstances, these sentiments may be articulated loudly or acted out. A bird's-eye view of the group at this stage would show each person or subgroup spaced as far away as possible from everyone else. Postures are stiff, rigid. Voices are brusque, clipped, tight. Distrust is rampant, confusion high. There is considerable tension, if not outright fighting.

During the *storming* stage of group development a lot of talented groups submerge, sometimes never to re-emerge. It is characterized by constant bickering, tension, passive aggression or subversion, outright battles, or all of the above. Even though the work is getting done—sort of—the main characteristics of group interaction are resistance, frustration and resentment. Hardly a pleasant work situation!

The storming stage is an obvious time to utilize Syntax skills. This stage *cannot* be skipped, but it *can* be minimized. It is one of the best examples of "going slow to go fast." Remembering to match before you lead, and to stay in the Aim Frame will help. If you are group leader, the best move you can make is to clearly delineate the task and its boundaries. To do this, ask questions about the goal. "Are we all clear about our goals in this project?" Such non-strident openings permit the group to shift attention from "Who has power?" to "What needs to be done?"

If that doesn't work, more must be done to build rapport and establish trust. How much time to spend settling these issues is a concern. Our rule of thumb is that the longer the group will be working together, the more time you should spend on front-end work. If the task is finite and brief, ironing out interpersonal issues is not a high priority. If the task is large and complex, time *not* spent resolving those issues up front will be spent ten-fold later on.

For all members, it is essential to remember that this stage is inevitable and therefore not to take it personally. The resistance reducers described in Chapter Seven are also very useful.

Norming

Having established clear, specific, shared goals, the group can establish operational norms—an understanding about how the work will get done and relationships managed. When group members are willing and able to do that, they have moved into the *norming* stage. This stage is less formally polite than the forming stage but not entirely relaxed. Voices are less stri-dent, body postures are less rigid, there is more give-and-take in the dia-logue, and humor reappears.

In this stage people start to play certain roles. One may play Devil's Advo-cate, another Peacemaker, while yet another may be Clock Watcher. They may not be their natural selves, but they are willing to play positive roles to get the work done. Consequently, the group leader can shift attention away from the task and towards managing relationships.

This is the stage at which questions about specifics can be especially use-ful. "What" and "how" questions make explicit each member's implicit as-sumptions. Limits probes uncover whether operational assumptions—"We can't do it that way," "Management feels we've failed," "Either we ship it tomorrow or we lose the contract," "We have to deliver by the day after tomorrow"—are based in reality or are a function of someone's mental map.

It is also the stage at which to employ clear requests and agreements. Use them to build norms that ensure clean contracts among all team members, as well as between the team and its customers. This will increase the team's capacity to re-balance as workloads shift and shift again. Patient attention to detail pays off with carefully crafted norms that every group member can fully support.

Performing

As working processes are negotiated, people begin visibly to relax. They shift attention back to the task itself and start to get things done. This is the *performing* stage, the "flow state" characterized by cooperation and accom-plishment. Leadership can be relinquished because everyone has accepted personal responsibility for getting the job done. Team members feel free to be their best selves. Exchanges are less polite and more natural. Work is accomplished with little wasted motion. Members enjoy each other's company and regularly seek each other out for support, feedback, encouragement, and shared learning.

In fact, this is the time most effectively to employ the skill of *learning*. With the safety net of the group, there is room to take risks, gather feedback, notice the results of actions taken, and make adjustments if actions do not produce what you want. A high-performing team creates an ideal set of conditions for learning and for sharing that learning.

Task and Relationship Maintenance

The process of group work confronts groups with two sets of interpersonal issues: facilitating the task's accomplishment and maintaining relationships. Both utilize Syntax skills extensively; the difference is their focus. When facilitating the *task,* effective group members and leaders do the following:

1. **Initiate:** Start the work process by defining the group's goal, capturing relevant group assumptions (and exploring them in depth if necessary), suggesting ways to manage the task by breaking it into "do-able" pieces, proposing a time line and creating subgroups to address different aspects of the task.

2. **Seek Information and Opinions:** Invite responses; gather sensory data and group wisdom on how to proceed; determine what issues and options might be faced; decide how best to handle logistical, procedural, social and political aspects of the task.

3. **Give Information and Opinions:** Share the information that has been gathered, and remember to distinguish sensory data from interpretation.

4. **Clarify and Elaborate:** Use verification skills to clear up ambiguous ideas or suggestions; identify the relationship between ideas and processes, and build on the ideas of others.

5. **Summarize:** Outline key points of the discussion to date; pull together common themes so the group can stay on track and move forward.

6. **Evaluate:** Ask group members to set measuring points at which to gauge progress in terms of content and relationships. One consulting group suggests frequent "process checks" (about every forty-five minutes) to determine what is working and not working for each member of the team.

7. **Test for Mutual Understanding:** Question members periodically to see if there is agreement on both task and process—what should be done and how it should be done. Determine the level of support—non-existent, lukewarm, or strong.

While all these behaviors contain strong interpersonal elements, their focus is on getting the work done. The *relationship* skills of effective group members and leaders are slightly different.

1. **Gatekeep:** Make sure all members contribute their full worth. Give introverted people enough time to ponder critical issues before they are asked to respond. See that speakers are not interrupted and, in general, allow all parties to be heard.

2. **Set and Maintain Standards:** Make sure that group norms are established, clarified, and maintained.

3. **Harmonize:** Don't resist resistance; instead, recognize and address the underlying concerns. Accept that the resistance represents useful information and determine its root sources.

4. **Encourage:** Provide support and feedback that demonstrates you value members' contributions and participation.[2]

These descriptions of the dynamics and work involved in effective teams are additional frames for you, more ways to systematically organize and apply intra- and interpersonal learning capabilities. Just like knowing the rules of baseball helps you enjoy watching a game, understanding these forces at work helps you relax and enjoy the team process. Knowing these rules has become essential for success in the New Workplace Game.

Conclusion

When you recognize the underlying structure of groups—including the team you are working on right now—and assess its stage of development, you have choices to make about how to proceed. You can apply your personal syntax to make working together a positive and productive experience for everyone. You recognize that your feelings and behavior are a natural part of the group process and acceptable in the New Workplace Game. You make moves that support positive group process. Because you engender successful team experiences by setting clear goals, building strong relationships, getting the job done, and learning well, you become the person everyone wants on their team.

---

[2] Adapted from the work of Sandra Mobley, The Learning Advantage, Arlington, VA.

CHAPTER FIFTEEN

Balancing Results and Relationships

Balance is *key* to effectiveness. What do we mean by balance? According to the dictionary, balance is a "state or position of equipoise, harmony or an aesthetically pleasing integration of elements, mental and emotional steadiness."[1]

Balance is the most resourceful state we can achieve, the one in which all our skills and abilities are most effectively applied. Some achieve balance in a steady-state way; others do it over time, swinging first in one direction and then in another. There is no right or wrong; it is simply an aspect of personal syntax.

Purpose

Throughout this book we have urged you to take responsibility for the results you get. Here is an important opportunity to put to work what you have learned. You, not us, will provide most of the content of this chapter. We will review the model and significant learning points from each of the other chapters. You will have opportunities to audit communication situations, think through your personal syntax, prepare for skill practice, and define a personal balance point from which to maintain equilibrium amid the turbulent waves of a twenty-first century career.

A Quick Review

You will recall our suggestion that human interactions form a system in which, like any other system, changes in one part ultimately affect the whole. There is only one aspect of the system you can control and that is yourself, or at least your behavior. While that frustrates many managers, it can also help them understand how to accomplish things with people.

---

[1] *Webster's Seventh New Collegiate Dictionary* (Springfield, Mass.: G. & C. Merriam Company, 1969) 66.

We explored The Law of Requisite Variety: "The element in the system with the most flexibility will ultimately gain the most control in the system." We believe this is as true in human communication systems as it is in neurological and automated control systems. In human communication, flexibility means having access to a wide range of behavior. Under pressure, however, most of us cannot generate a lot of new behaviors. We are much more likely to behave differently at the critical moment if we give advance thought to what the new behavior might be.

Just as in languages, whether spoken or programming, behavior has an underlying structure or syntax. Individuals have a personal syntax, group dynamics have a syntax, and effective interpersonal behavior has a clear syntax. We introduced that syntax as the Syntax of Effectiveness, with the skill sets of PLAN, LINK, INFORM, and LEARN. The axes of the model highlight the dynamics of FOCUS and FLEXIBILITY. The use of effective requests and agreements help establish BALANCE between the two.

The skills of PLAN include the creation of a clear purpose and desirable future state, both for yourself and the groups you work in. In LINK, you establish rapport and learn to handle resistance positively and usefully. In INFORM, with a deep appreciation of the complex filters through which you process information, you ask questions that elicit clean, undistorted information. In LEARN, you shift attention to the feedback you constantly get about how you are doing. You also remember to appreciate the many ways people learn and grow, and utilize effective requests and agreements to establish the flow through which work gets done.

Throughout, we have stressed that context is crucial. You have acquired tools—not learned rules—because you are constantly adjusting to the reality of the moment. This is especially true when you work in teams, taking into account stages of team development as well as personal patterns.

The Syntax Model offers a clear and systematic framework for diagnosing and repairing communication breakdowns. It also provides a frame in which effective communicators establish personal balance. Using it as a diagnostic tool, you can determine whether your emphasis is weighted too heavily towards flexibility or towards focus. Both are necessary: Balance allows you to pace yourself for the long haul. Total flexibility without focus will wear you out, and total focus without flexibility will burn everyone else out. Each of us has a unique balance point, and no balance point stays fixed over time.

Remember, human communication systems are fundamentally complex and non-linear. Cause and effect are not always clear and predictable. Interestingly, human behavior is one of the more stable and predictable subsystems of an increasingly complex work environment! When you know how to consciously learn and grow your skills in that subsystem, you master the skills for success in the New Workplace Game.

Designing Balance

Throughout *Smart Work,* we have emphasized that you have a lot of choice about behaviors you may have thought to be beyond your control. For many, having a balance in their lives is one of those areas: "It's great when it happens, and it's not my fault if I lose it. Life's just too unpredictable." Life is certainly unpredictable, but you may have more choice than you think. The goal of this chapter is to help you to identify and focus your current balance point. The following worksheets encourage you to think about what it takes for you to maintain your equilibrium when the world appears to have none. When you know what you require to be in balance, you can more proactively create those conditions.

The process of this chapter is as follows: First, use the Audit in Figure 15-1 to review the Syntax of Effectiveness as it occurs in your communication situations. Then think through the Personal Syntax questions (Figure 15-2), noting strengths and growth opportunities in each area. The goal-setting questions (Figure 15-3) will help you create your own work-related statement of balance. Prioritizing skills to develop and making the commitment to practice them is the final step (Figure 15-4).

To prepare for the Syntax Communication Audit, identify three communication situations in which you are currently engaged. Enter a key word at the top of each column to indicate the situation. Use the fourth column to generalize about your syntax. In answering the questions, think only about whether these behaviors occur, not whose "fault" it is if they do not. Use the rating scale to identify top priorities for those situations and for yourself.

Use this profile to set learning goals, checking periodically on your progress.

For each column, list a communication situation that affects your effectiveness at work. Fill in the number that best describes each situation, then total the results across and down.

Scoring: 1___ 2___ 3___ 4___ 5

    Rarely   Sometimes   Usually

	1
PLAN—Do you	
Maintain a positive climate for communicating?	
Develop common goals and objectives?	
Make objectives clear and observable?	
LINK—Do you	
Cooperate and work as a team?	
Base relationships on mutual trust?	
Manage disagreement with mutual respect?	
INFORM—Do you	
Exchange information accurately?	
Check out interpretations and distortions?	
Verify and follow-up?	
LEARN—Do you	
Take actions as agreed upon?	
Remain open to receiving feedback?	
Provide feedback consistently?	
BALANCE—Do you	
Pay attention to both task and relationship?	
Make complete, clear requests?	
Accept, decline, and renegotiate agreements?	
TOTAL by situation	

Based on these scores, what situation and what skill are your priorities for improvement?

1. Situation: _____

2. Skill: _____

FIGURE 15-1: SYNTAX COMMUNICATION AUDIT

2	3	4	TOTALS by skill:
		Overall (your personal syntax)	Add columns 1–4 across

The questions in Figure 15-2 explore your personal syntax. Note where you currently feel strongest and where you see opportunities for growth.

PLAN

I regularly set clear and compelling goals for myself; I know what I want, what it will get me, and how I will know I have achieved it.

I check to see if it is exactly what I want and if anything is missing.

I revisit my goals frequently and adjust them as needed.

Strengths:

Opportunities for Growth:

FIGURE 15-2A: HOW AM I DOING?—PLAN

LINK

I am capable of establishing rapport with a wide range of people and do so regularly and naturally.

I become consciously aware of and utilize rapport skills when I am not achieving the relationship quality I want.

I remember that resistance is information and don't take it personally. I respond with genuine concern and curiosity, and I can consistently reduce the resistance I encounter.

Strengths:

Opportunities for Growth:

FIGURE 15-2B: HOW AM I DOING?—LINK

INFORM

I compensate for the natural tendency to delete, distort, and generalize by asking specifics and limits questions.

I remember to seek sensory data so that I can make up my own mind, and provide sensory data so that others may do the same.

I remember to maintain rapport when seeking information.

Strengths:

Opportunities for Growth:

FIGURE 15-2C: HOW AM I DOING?—INFORM

LEARN

I accept feedback about my performance and adjust my behavior accordingly.

I know how I learn best, and consciously position myself to maximize learning in every new situation.

I review the past as "feedback" not "failure."

I use curiosity to drive out fear and help me enjoy the learning process.

Strengths:

Opportunities for Growth:

FIGURE 15-2D: HOW AM I DOING?—LEARN

FOCUS

I set goals and take action to achieve them, checking regularly to see that the goals are on track and noticing whether my actions move me toward the goal.

Strengths:

Opportunities for Growth:

FIGURE 15-2E: HOW AM I DOING?—FOCUS

FLEXIBILITY

I easily shift attention from tasks to relationships, making sure I address others' issues.

I pay attention to the responses from others and adjust my communication accordingly.

Strengths:

Opportunities for Growth:

FIGURE 15-2F: HOW AM I DOING?—FLEXIBILITY

BALANCE

I keep task and relationship in balance without losing sight of my goals.

I use clear requests and agreements as tools to maintain balance.

I continually learn and take pleasure in knowing I am an effective person.

Strengths:

Opportunities for Growth:

FIGURE 15-2G: HOW AM I DOING?—BALANCE

As you review your Figure 15-2 notes, think about what is working well for you and what isn't. Which of your behaviors help keep you balanced, and which probably contribute to your losing balance? Then go ahead and fill out the next worksheet, Figure 15-3.

What I want in order to achieve personal balance in my work:

What that will get me:

Summary statement:

When I have it, I will see:

And I will hear:

And my emotional state will be:

FIGURE 15-3: GOAL—PERSONAL BALANCE

The Ongoing Balancing Act

Are you thinking "Whoa, this is getting ridiculous! Why do I have to pay this much attention to balance?" Read this passage from *Fortune:*

> *"Pay attention to your inner self. You can't win if you're dead of a heart attack or maddened by stress. So exercise. Meditate. Make love. Build a tree house. Do something selfless. Global competition demands the best of you. Getting centered has never been more important."*[2]

In your twenties and early thirties, you can accomplish much with sheer will power. When you are older, however, economies of motion—simple and elegant solutions to the problems of everyday living—make more and more sense.

Balance is the ultimate expression of economy of motion. It establishes clear goals you can use to prioritize and allocate time and energy, the skills with which to analyze and adapt to your environment, and the momentum to act and continue to learn. Anything less diminishes your capabilities and performance.

Building in the Daily Practice

Once you have identified specific Syntax skills to work on, how do you proceed? How do you develop a given skill? This list offers possibilities, many developed over the years by our seminar participants. It is by no means comprehensive. These are starting points—use them to trigger even more imaginative ideas of your own.

---

[2] "Seven Steps to Being the Best," *Fortune,* 13 December 1993.

IF YOU WANT TO WORK ON: **DO THIS:**

FUNDAMENTALS (see Chapter Two)

Diagnostics *(figuring out what is going wrong and how to correct it quickly)*

Post the Model somewhere easy to see, so that you can quickly figure out the source of breakdown, sort through possibilities, and try something new.

PLAN (see Chapters Four, Five & Seven)

Aim & Blame

Ask yourself: "Am I talking about what I *do* want or what I *don't* want?" Consciously omit "but" from your vocabulary for three to six weeks. Replace it with "and."

Goal Questions

To uncover embedded goals, ask "What will that get me/them?" every time you hear or set a goal.

Develop "fully specified outcomes" for even seemingly trivial goals. Ask: "How will I/they know? What will I/they see? Hear? Feel? Say?"

Sensory v. Interpretive

When bored in meetings, study: patterns of eye movements—what do the eyes do when people are remembering? Learning? Deciding? Study patterns of muscle movement around the eyes; patterns of muscle movement around the mouth; patterns of body alignment. Note any correlation to the way decisions are made?

Listen to the way words reflect the way people process information (visual, auditory, or kinesthetic).

Practice with friends: What do their faces look like when they're thinking "Yes?" "No?" Learn to pay conscious attention to the subtle indicators of internal states (which you already do unconsciously)—it will help you separate fact from interpretation.

LINK (Chapters Six & Seven)

Rapport

Consciously use non-verbal leads before verbal ones for three to six weeks.

Resistance Reducers

Pick one resistance reducer and use it as often as appropriate for a week; then move on to the next. Focus on one at a time; after a while they'll all flow easily and naturally.

INFORM (Chapters Eight, Nine & Ten)

Specifics

Delete "why" from your vocabulary for three to six weeks and develop other ways to elicit the same information more precisely and quickly. Practice asking questions that uncover all unspecified data bits at one time, for example, "Who, specifically, said what to whom?"

Limits

Pick one limits probe and use it (when you hear the cues) regularly for a week. Then move to the next, down the list.

Verification

Practice verifying EVERYTHING for three to six weeks. To acquire a wide range of options, develop one or two new phrases to use each week.

LEARN (Chapters Eleven, Twelve & Fifteen)

Take Action

Set up a systematic plan for improving interpersonal effectiveness and enter specific actions in your calendar/organizer. Prioritize for specific situations.

Get Feedback	Ask friends for feedback! Be specific about what you're working on.
	Notice when you're not getting the results you want and STOP. Don't do anything more for the first week. Think of alternatives, and then DO SOMETHING DIFFERENT.
BALANCE (Chapters Thirteen & Fifteen)	
Requests	Analyze requests, checking for the structure of complete requests at least three times a day for a week. Write down what you observe.
	In meetings and conversations, ask "What is your request?" and verify what you hear.
	Make two requests more per day than usual.
Responses	Run through the four options (agree, decline, counteroffer, commit to commit) before responding to a request.
	Practice making responses that are difficult for you (for example, declining or renegotiating) five times a week for three weeks.

Now use Figure 15-4 to help identify your priorities for learning. After reviewing your notes, decide what kind of improvements would net the most gain. What investment of time and attention would get the most "bang for the buck?" What are you actually willing to commit to doing?

Based on my assessments and the suggested drills, I commit myself to practicing the following skills:

1. _____

2. _____

3. _____

How I will begin this week:

1. Action _____

   Situation _____

2. Action _____

   Situation _____

3. Action _____

   Situation _____

I will perform a progress check on _____. [*Enter this date in your calendar now!*]

FIGURE 15-4: PRIORITIES FOR LEARNING

The Hard Work of Self-Development

The decision to change your behavior reflects commitment to the kind of "personal mastery" discussed in Chapter Twelve. As you replace old unproductive behaviors with new, fruitful ones, be very patient with yourself. **Work on one thing at a time** or you will overload. Here are some important points to remember:

- **It takes three to six weeks of consistent practice to change habits.** Changing them at the default level—so new behaviors are accessible in crises when you need them the most—may take years;

- **Notice your improvement**, in whatever increments it occurs. Keep asking yourself "What's different now from when I started?" Spend regular time on the observation deck reviewing your efforts and thinking about how it might have been without the changes.

- **Appreciate your progress.** Accept compliments from friends and colleagues as your effectiveness increases. Note how curiosity can replace fear and keep life on a more even keel. Observe how much more enjoyable life becomes when you seek positive solutions rather than excuses for failure, possess a clear sense of purpose and direction, connect effortlessly with other people, stop getting blindsided by missing or incorrect information, and constantly learn new and fascinating things.

People who are effective manage their attention and their learning process so they can move forward without overloading.

Conclusion

We have now reached the conclusion of *Smart Work*. You have been exposed to a variety of mindsets and tools that will support the new ways of working that the twenty-first century will require. Really, however, you've now reached the beginning. From here on out the story is yours to tell: Do you try out the behaviors? Do you notice the differences in your results? Are they the ones you wanted? Do you keep experimenting, fine tuning, calibrating, becoming ever more clear, direct, precise, and elegant in your excellence as a communicator?

And do you recognize your own need for balance, and know how to regain it? Balance is hard-won in our complex, busy lives. Achieving it today does not guarantee we will have it tomorrow when we may need it even more. Even highly effective people struggle for balance. Everybody practices the behaviors described in *Smart Work* once in a while, and effective people practice them most frequently. That's what makes them more resilient, more focused, better balanced, and in general more successful.

We have given you a framework, a set of tools and concepts to increase your overall satisfaction with work and life, and to bring both into balance. Our wish is that we have cleared up the mysteries of the New Workplace Game, helped you perceive the underlying framework of your own effectiveness, encouraged your curiosity about undertaking continuous learning about people, and made useful the insights we have developed in years of helping technical and professional people get the results they want. Our work is over; yours is just beginning. A lifetime of fascinating field study and exploration awaits you. Enjoy it!

Index

frames, 23–30
  aim, 26, 28
  blame, 25, 63
  outcome, 26
  problem, 25
Fritz, Robert, 106
future
  action, 122
  check, 35

G

Gardner, Howard, 100
Gaster, David, 7
generalization, 71, 107
gestures, 48
goals, 150
  setting, 31–42
  shared, 10
group development, 129–135
  forming, 131
  norming, 133
  performing, 133
  storming, 132
Grinder, John, 92

H

handling resistance, 13, 57, 61
Hoffer, Eric, 84
hot buttons, 61

I

impossibles, 82, 85
INFORM, 12, 67, 81, 138, 144, 151
intelligence, 100
  interpersonal, 100
  intrapersonal, 101
  kinesthetic, 101
  linguistic, 100
  logical, 101
  mathematical, 101
  musical, 101
  practical, 100

spatial, 101
verbal, 100
visual, 101
interpersonal intelligence, 101
interpretation, 67
intrapersonal intelligence, 101

K

kinesthetic intelligence, 101
kinesthetic processing, 92, 96–98
Kline, Peter, 102

L

language
  body, 95
  of agreement, 119
  of requests, 119, 125
  sensory-based, 72
Law of Requisite Variety, 111
leadership, 41
leading too soon, 61
LEARN, 6, 12, 99, 102–108,
  109–118, 138, 145, 151
learning
  double-loop, 27, 104, 105, 108,
    109, 116
  priorities, 103, 153
  single-loop, 26, 104, 116
  styles, 103
limits, 81–87, 151
limits probes, 81–87, 151
linguistic intelligence, 100
LINK, 12, 138, 143, 151
listener, 46, 123
listening, 43, 46, 52
logical intelligence, 101

M

manipulation, 47
maps, 21, 63, 75, 82, 84
matching, 48, 61
  before leading, 61

personal learning, 109, 118
self assessment, 142

T

taking the lead, 52
task, 130, 134
teams, 41, 129–135
thinking, 15, 20, 45
threat, 26, 57
time, 69, 124
TQM, 29
Tuckman, Bruce, 131

U

universals, 82, 85

V

verbal intelligence, 100
verification, 41, 61, 87–89
vision/values, 5
visual, 92–98
visual-spatial intelligence, 101
voice tone and tempo, 48

W

Welch, Jack, 7
why, 15, 76–77